HOW TO HELP YOUR CHILD COPE WITH ANYTHING

Dr Alison McClymont is a UK-registered clinical psychologist, specialising in trauma, she is also UK accredited as an arts therapist. She has over 15 years' experience working with children and adolescents in a wide range of settings, including secure CAMHS units, NGOs and special education settings. Alison has worked as a guest lecturer at the University of Hong Kong and a clinical supervisor for counselling students, and has run a trauma recovery programme for refugee children and families. Alison has worked in private practice in Hong Kong, Brazil and has now returned to the UK to continue working in private practice with trauma survivors.

Alison's doctoral studies focused on trauma recovery for child victims of trafficking, and her previous research has looked at the impact of vicarious trauma in first responders, and the impact of parenting styles in trauma recovery. Alison's passion is helping survivors of trauma find a path to recovery and healing, and she is trained in a number of therapeutic modalities, including EMDR, CBT and schema therapy.

When not following her passion of working with patients, she is at home with her two dogs and her two children.

HOW TO HELP YOUR CHILD COPE WITH ANYTHING

A PARENT'S GUIDE TO ANXIETY, BULLYING AND THE HURDLES OF EARLY CHILDHOOD

DR ALISON McCLYMONT

S

First published in Great Britain in 2024 by Orion Spring
an imprint of The Orion Publishing Group Ltd
Carmelite House, 50 Victoria Embankment
London EC4Y 0DZ

An Hachette UK Company

1 3 5 7 9 10 8 6 4 2

A CIP catalogue record for this book is
available from the British Library.

Every effort has been made to ensure that the information in this book is accurate. The
information in this book may not be applicable in each individual case, so it is advised
that professional medical advice is obtained for specific health matters and before
changing any medication or dosage. Neither the publisher nor author accepts any legal
responsibility for any personal injury or other damage or loss arising from the use of the
information in this book. In addition, if you are concerned about your diet or exercise
regime and wish to change them, you should consult a health practitioner first.

ISBN (Trade Paperback) 978 1 3987 2093 0
ISBN (eBook) 978 1 3987 2094 7
ISBN (Audio) 978 1 3987 2095 4

Typeset by Input Data Services Ltd, Bridgwater, Somerset

Printed in Great Britain by Clays Ltd, Elcograf S.p.A.

MIX
Paper | Supporting
responsible forestry
FSC
www.fsc.org **FSC® C104740**

www.orionbooks.co.uk

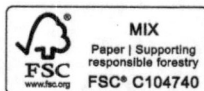

CONTENTS

To Issy and Tabbi . . . And the garden of yellow flowers

A NOTE FROM THE AUTHOR

No parent is born, all are created through experience, history and emotional education. Every parent had a parent, and they had a parent, and they had a parent, and they had a parent – you get the idea; parenting is a 'triggering' experience. Your boundaries are constantly being tested and it is draining both physically and emotionally, but by learning to understand how our past is shaping our future we can break negative patterns and reframe them to become the parent we wish to be. We can also enhance our own emotional literacy to help, support and enable the next generation to clearly navigate their emotions and feelings.

I have dedicated my professional career to researching trauma theories and the biology of the brain. I feel passionately that if people could learn to be more familiar with this system, they would understand themselves, and others, a lot more. I have found that teaching people about their nervous system and their biological emotional response has brought clarity and insight in a way that simple talking therapy couldn't reach.

With children, I have found it is even more crucial to understand how their brains react to emotions, in order to ensure their brain develops in a healthy way. In this book we will explore the ways that difficult experiences can impact memory, and how this might affect future relationships or situations. I hope in reading this book you learn how to regulate your nervous system to stay as calm and happy as you want to be, and how to assist your child when their brain is in survival mode or overwhelm.

It's not an uncommon parenting challenge to be faced with your child saying, 'This happened, what now?' and feeling utterly stumped for what to say or do next. We have been socially conditioned to only celebrate the 'pretty' emotions: happiness, gratitude, joy and love, so we are primed to want to look away when the 'ugly' emotions of shame, disgust and anger rear their heads. It is almost counterintuitive to sit in the chaos, the hopelessness, the envy and the anger, so we unconsciously reject them; we simply choose to move away. But as a therapist to trauma survivors, I have learnt that to not attempt to plaster over someone's story, or reject it, is the true act of empathising with another.

I wanted to write this book to acknowledge that it's OK if you don't know how to heal your child's pain, but I'd like to give you the tools I've learnt both for myself and for my patients to help you try.

And none of us had perfect parents who gave us a foolproof example to follow. If you think you did, I'd love to meet you, as I have never met a perfect parent, and I have never met a perfect child. I hope that in reading this you will find a space to sit with the 'ugly' emotions in both yourself and your child, and realise those emotions aren't that ugly at all – they just need a friend.

With love, Dr Alison

INTRODUCTION

No parent wants to consider that there might be times where we can't just 'fix it'. We want to believe that for every scraped knee, every head bump, every tearful altercation, we will be there. As children grow up and emotional interactions become more complicated, we might face even more challenging experiences, such as our child being bullied, or even bullying another child. All of these playground memories can stir up our own buried feelings and hidden past experiences. Someone once described to me that watching their child leave their arms and walk into a playground was like watching their heart walk outside of their body. Our child carries with them all of our emotions about being a child, being a parent, and being human. We pour so much of our life into these little beings that it can feel the greatest moment of vulnerability to watch them leave our loving protection and go into the big wide world.

This becomes even harder as our children start attending nursery or school, where maybe for the first time they find themselves in social situations that we can't help them navigate. This is a normal struggle for both the developing child and the developing parent – when do we intervene in a dispute with another child and when do we let things runs their course? General advice ranges from letting them sort it out themselves to getting stuck in and mediating – so what do we do? Do we stand back and let the social learning commence without us, or do we get in the thick of it and show them that we are alongside them in every difficult aspect of growing up? If we do this, will they feel supported and nurtured, or will we deny them that all-important social skill of resilience?

There's no straightforward answer to this and, as we read all the time in parenting media, every child is different. Like adults, some children find navigating social situations much more difficult than others, and as any parent of a neurodiverse child will tell you, social interactions with others can be a painful and anxiety-creating experience.

I am a psychologist, trauma specialist and creative arts therapist with over 15 years' experience working with the complete spectrum of childhood adversity – from big T traumas (abuse, domestic violence, war, natural disasters) to little t traumas (bullying, family financial instability, family mental health issues, divorce, bereavement).

I have seen, through my work and my research, the lasting impact of childhood experiences on later adulthood. I have also seen that the majority of child psychology books that refer to trauma are referring to what I call big T trauma, but what about the stress of divorce, bereavement, blended families, multiple house or school moves? Why do we not talk about them?

Life happens, divorce happens, and bereavement happens, all of which may be outside of our control. But the purpose of this book is to help you, the parent, to plant, nurture and tend a solid foundation that will encourage your child to flourish into a healthy, emotionally resilient adult. This book is here to help you to help your little ones find the words, images and actions to relay their internal experience to the adults in their life, and it's also designed to help you navigate these uncharted waters, by improving your own emotional literacy and your understanding of a child's developing brain.

This generation of parents face many challenges that previous generations of parents didn't have to battle. Now more than ever there is targeted messaging designed to interact with our children in a way that has never been seen before. This generation of children are exposed to 554 brands a DAY, and a recent study (Stacy-Jo Dickson: 2023) suggested that 24 per cent of children between 3 and 4 have a social media profile, and that rises to 91 per cent by the time the children hit the 12–15 age bracket. From a political perspective, while wider government studies suggest that children coped broadly 'well' with the pandemic, the under-7 age group was one of the hardest hit, with missed academic targets most widely reported in reception-aged children. Parenting in a post-pandemic world truly is, to quote an overused phrase, unprecedented times.

As a mother of two young children, I know that while everything is perfect in research, nothing is perfect in life, and we won't get everything right all of the time. That's OK. I hope that you, the parent or caregiver, pick up this book and find within it an empowering message that helps you to parent your children through challenges and adversity with love, empathy and compassion.

Throughout this book you will get to learn more about your child's brain and how experiences, both positive and negative, can affect them. We will also explore in detail the idea of attachment, and how our attachment pattern works as a blueprint for our future relationships. Then we will journey into the heart of the 'problem', exploring these little t traumas in depth, and come to learn how they can impact a child.

I want you to use this book as not just a learning tool but also an interactive manual for how to respond in the event your child experiences something that hurts. So there will be tools to help you engage with the subject matter, including my own technique of Extract–Express–Reflect, and many more from my play therapy toolbox and my psychology room.

ODE TO THE MODERN MOTHER

I want to take a moment to single out the particular experience of the modern mother. The modern mother, I would argue, has never been so isolated and yet so maligned. She is exhausted, she is under pressure and she is berated from all angles. I accept that no generation of mothers have had it easy, and this generation has benefited from many things that have removed some of the manual labour of child rearing (washing machines, disposable nappies, microwaves etc.); however, the modern mother has run the gamut of mixed messaging about how to parent. It began in the 1940s when Dr Truby King told parents that everything had to be done on a schedule, and if the schedule wasn't adhered to perfectly you had spoilt your child. There were some very practical reasons for this style of parenting at the time – life was hard, a number of things had to be done by hand and the 'mother load' came with a lot of manual labour. But the invention explosion of household appliances in the 1950s brought along with it the psychology of Dr Spock, who told mothers to stop doing the laundry and to cuddle their child – this was now the most essential part of mothering.

This was then bulldozed by some big names in 'science', who told mothers that actually that was the worst thing they could be doing, and what they needed to strive for was 'programming operant behaviour'. As championed by B.F. Skinner, parents were now told that parenting was simply a procedure of rewarding the behaviours you wanted to encourage and punishing those that you didn't.

Then in the 1970s we circled all the way back to attachment parenting, where the parent was the most important figure for the child, and this has been later extrapolated into promoting ideas of baby-led weaning / baby wearing / co-sleeping. But in the 1980s we met the woman who was supposed to 'have it all': she was now supposed to take her place in the boardroom and in the aerobics studio at an age when the body beautiful was as important as career success. Alongside these things she had to run a beautiful, well-kept household; she was told that it was all a nonsense that you had to choose career or home – do both!

The 1990s mum was warned of the dangers of becoming her '80s sister, the 'career mum' and was told she had to go back to family values. She had to protect and nurture her children to the point she was sometimes called the 'helicopter mum' – a parent who was told they should put the needs and happiness of the child above all things, and never should the child experience upset or unhappiness. This mother was told she had to take such an active role in the social and emotional development of her child that she buzzed around them (hence the helicopter term). This was the age of the first parent-led and parent-supervised 'play date'. Gone are the days when mothers told children to sort their own conflicts out; now mothers had to play coach and referee.

Then we come to the 2000s, when mothers were supposed to go back to nature; non-medicalised birth became a term and organic, baby-led weaning was promoted. But now we enter the beginnings of the age of divided parenting groups, with so many parenting attitudes and styles around we see an age of debate and parenting 'stances'. Those who 'do Gina Ford', those who 'do Sears', those who want to be an SAHM (stay-at-home mum) or a 'working mum'. Social media starts taking off in this decade and forums such as Mumsnet become both a source of comfort and of self-punishment. The mummy WhatsApp group takes off and parents find themselves in a sea of judgement, advice, 'helpful critique' and stealth bragging. The modern mother finds herself in an age of 'sharenting' – when sharing your parenting with the online world is the norm, and your social media feed swells with mum-fluencers just waiting to tell you what to do / what not to do / how to edit it.

In this later age of parenting dictats, we saw dads getting pulled into the furore of complex parenting messages: *Are you a provider? Great! But are you also a great father? Are you a father who prioritises family time? Did you take paternity leave? Did you attend the antenatal classes? Do you support your partner emotionally, physically and socially? Are you a feminist? Did you attend the birth? Do you 'imaginary play'? In fact, do you imaginary play so well that the dad from Bluey the cartoon show is your spirt animal? Did you do the night feeds? Do you do the school pick-ups? Did you watch the tutorial on how to braid hair? Do you post all of the above on social media?*

All of the above? Wonderful! But hold on ... You are a good provider, right? You still make sure that age-old adage of 'bringing home the bacon' is attended to? But of course, don't be TOO work obsessed, be a father, above all things, be a father ... a father who provides. Yes, I mean financially ... but also a father.

The modern parent has never faced a greater barrage of messaging of how to 'parent well'. Once upon a time, only mothers were dragged into this toxic dialogue, but now we see more and more fathers being pulled in also. I suspect grandparents are just over the horizon as the next targets that parenting media wants to shame, blame and train. This morning I took a quick scroll on my social media and I found the following messages in the contents just dying to tell me what I as a modern mother should do in order to be 'successful':

Cots are terrible. Cots come in a number of ergonomic, expensive and aesthetically pleasing designs. But cots are terrible. But then again co-sleeping is fatal . . .

Dummies will cause dental issues, and will prevent 'natural' attachment patterns of breastfeeding . . . oh, and breastfeeding? If you choose to do that, then good for you, but not too long, or that's weird . . . The food you feed your children? Better be organic and from a locally produced source or you are not only denying your child's immune system its vital nutrients, you are also furthering climate change.

Then let's get into your post-natal body – better get that back quickly, but not too quickly, oh and don't talk to your daughter about your body or she might get an eating disorder; but have a perfect body. Did you get that? Get that perfect body, don't talk about it, or work for it, in fact don't mention it, but have it . . . you need to have it, OK? Because otherwise fashion will reject you and you will be seen as unfeminine, but don't let the sisterhood down by getting obsessed with it, OK? But get it, get your body back . . . just be quiet about it. Above all, though: have a GREAT body.

Oh, and let's get into schools . . . are you going private? Good for you, your child will benefit from the smaller class sizes . . .

but don't talk about that because we should all be going to state schools. Yes, we need to be more socially conscious and send our children to a school that represents a cross-section of society.

OK great, now let's discuss academic achievement for your kids – better get that. Because otherwise your child will fall behind and they will never get a job and they will starve in a garret, but don't be pushy with it, OK. Don't be 'tiger mother' about it, as that's damaging. Make sure they have outside interests. Lots of them, and they cost a lot, but that's fine because you can work and afford that, right?

What's more important than developing your child's interests? Don't work too much, as you need to be home nurturing your child . . . OK, anyway, back to the extra-curricular, make sure you are not pigeonholing them and make sure they are not being too pushed, but hopefully they will develop mastery of something. What's mastery? Oh, that's when you get really, really good at something, like Olympic-level good. Do you need to practise for hours to get there? Sure! And yes, that will cost time and money, but make sure you do that. Encouraging mastery is a great thing to do, and you must do it.

You work, right? You have a job, yes? Good . . . We don't want you just sitting around here doing nothing, that's anti-feminist. But don't be 'too much work', OK? Don't be like that, because who is going to make all the organic food!?! And who is going to do the after-school reading and make the costumes for the school plays?

Oh, and social media – stay well away from that, but just FYI there's a load of other perfect mothers on here just dying to show you what they did today and it's significantly more than you. And that perfect body . . . they have that. Those golden family times? They did that. How, you ask?? Easy – they just found a job to fit into THEIR lifestyle as a perfect mother and pay them a small fortune; sure, they get lambasted by every choice they make, but so what? They are rich and that's what matters, and having a perfect body . . . never forget that part.

While the above may seem amusing and light-hearted, consider this next to the statistic that 15 per cent of all mothers will experience postnatal depression. Now consider that figure skyrocketed to 35 per cent of mothers during the pandemic (Harrison et al: 2023), when social media use reached its record peak, with the average UK adult spending 4 hours a day online (Ofcom: 2023). The Priory UK in their study of the impact of social media 'sharenting' found that 40 per cent of new parents found that looking at idealised motherhood images online directly contributed to their feelings of depression and anxiety.

Parenting psychology has run the gamut over the last 100 years from telling parents to never cuddle their child for fear of creating dependence, to telling them cuddling is the most important thing you can do. Then we had the rise of behavioural analysis that told parents what they need to do is 'condition' behaviour through reward and removal systems, and lastly we had a new age of attachment parenting that told parents that the only way forward was baby wearing and co-sleeping.

All of these theories often form the basis of the breastfeeding vs formula debate, the stay-at-home mother vs the working mother debate, the sleep training vs co-sleeping debate, and everything in between. But secure attachment is not a formula, it is a relationship created through kind, consistent parenting. I am here to tell you that you can create a secure attachment with a bottle as much as with a breast. You can be a working mother who meets her child's emotions with empathy and kindness, and yes you can use a cot, or co-sleep, without causing irreparable brain damage.

I wish we could stop seeking out every excuse to bash parents over the head for their parenting choices. Even more, I wish we would stop doing this under the label of 'psychology' or, more ominously, just 'science'. Because while I don't know how to be a perfect mother, I know from over a decade's experience as a therapist that one way to create attachment challenges is to set a mother up with such high expectations of herself that when she cannot achieve them, she views her child's needs as demanding, and starts to resent them. Or the mother that tells herself if she just follows all the 'science' she WILL be perfect, and this parenting malarkey will all just tick along nicely with no spillages, but then feels a failure when she realises that parenting is a messier business than that. Parenting is not meant to be easy, it never has been. I'm sure ancient Egyptians experienced – alongside the joy – the exhaustion, tedium and confusion of parenting. Some time during the process you will meet parts of yourself that make you feel ashamed, disgusted or angry. This is OK! This does not make you a poor mother, a bad mother, a failure of a mother – it makes you a normal mother.

CHAPTER 1: WHAT IS TRAUMA?

This book is designed to help you understand what happens in your child's brain during the day-to-day struggles they might face in the playground, at school and at home. When we can understand the science of our child's brain responses, we can help them to navigate these situations in a calm 'brain state', rather than an activated 'stress state'. This book will focus on what I call the 'little t traumas', in other words the common experiences parents might find themselves managing on a regular basis — friendship struggles, sibling dynamics, encountering unfamiliar or frightening situations. When we teach children to navigate these little t traumas from a calm brain state we can help to prepare them for some of the bigger challenges life may throw at them.

One of the things I find most rewarding about working with

trauma responses is that it has a biological basis, and therefore responds well to treatment. I want to arm you with the information about how something called the parasympathetic nervous system works and how this system impacts the way traumatic memories are stored. When we understand this process we can help ourselves and others to release trauma from the body and decrease its relevance to us.

NEUROBIOLOGY OF EMOTION AND MEMORY

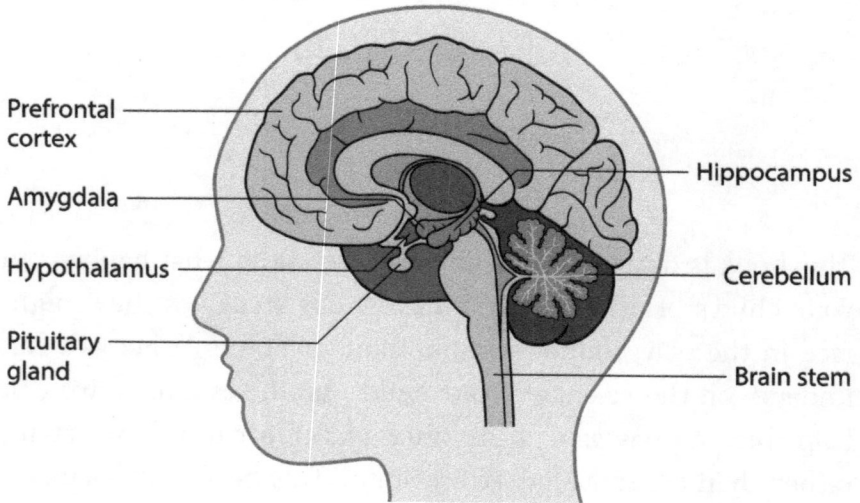

There is still a lot of debate around how memory actually functions, but it is generally agreed that our sensory organs (eyes / ears etc.) send messages to the prefrontal cortex and this information is then sent to the hippocampus: the memory bank. At the same time, our emergency response system, the amygdala, sends adrenaline and hormones related to joy and sadness to the memory bank.

It is important to remember that memories may be split into explicit (ones you can voice out loud) and implicit (ones that form part of the unconscious and are harder to retell). We do not store all information into memory, as that would be impossible; we need to filter what is worth keeping. So information goes through the short-term memory filter and the brain decides if it needs to be stored for later recall.

There is a lot of discussion around how this filtering process goes on. Some theories suggest that the more emotion attributed to a memory at the point of arriving in the hippocampus (the birth of a child, the death of a loved one, or your own wedding), the more likely it is to get filtered to the long-term memory. When it does store the memory for later recall, the brain, being a very efficient machine, codes this memory with the other data it received at the time, such as the hormone and adrenaline responses, and files all this neatly, like a library system.

THE TRAUMATISED CHILD'S BRAIN

When we consider the knowledge that the brain is not fully developed until 25, it is absolutely crucial to understand that childhood trauma can delay the development of the brain, or even cause damage to it. This is particularly true of traumas which occur before the age of three, because it is thought that pre-verbal trauma is harder for the brain to file accurately.

To explain this in real terms, MRI images of children who have suffered extreme trauma, such as abuse or neglect, show a smaller hippocampus than non-abused children. What this means is that their general memory function is impacted, as they experienced a trauma while their 'coding system' was developing, and it caused a glitch in the software.

The prefrontal cortex that controls impulse, reaction and judgement has also been seen to be altered or damaged, and the amygdala is overactive in the MRI scans of traumatised children. Why? Because the threat the child experienced at the time of the trauma caused the amygdala to flood the brain with adrenaline and the prefrontal cortex didn't know how to manage this. An adult brain with the same experience is less likely to send such an adrenaline flood, as it is a more fully developed, efficient system. But in a young brain these system malfunctions cause a short circuit.

When a developing brain hasn't had the opportunity to grow as it should, children are more prone to mental health issues. Children's brains adapt to the environment around them in order to survive; for example, a child whose amygdala was overactive due to witnessing violence in the home grows up to be hypervigilant, or is over-responsive to danger cues. Or a child who has been neglected may, due to their poor prefrontal cortex function which controls their impulses, be more prone to negative outbursts or ADHD.

In order to understand the way damage can occur in the brain, we need to understand how children can respond to traumatic stimuli, and for this we are going to take a deeper-dive science lesson (stay with me!) into neuropsychology and the polyvagal nerve.

POLYVAGAL THEORY

The polyvagal nerve runs from the brain stem down into the abdomen and controls digestion, breathing and heart rate (the parasympathetic nervous system). Polyvagal theory suggests that alongside the emotional centre of the limbic system, the vagus nerve is a key component in understanding the neurobiology of trauma. It supposes that our body is always working in one of three states: the ventral state, the sympathetic state or the dorsal state.

Ventral state

This is where we all want to be: the heart rate is normal, breathing relaxed, digestion is working as it should and the brain is transmitting and receiving messages in a normal manner.

Sympathetic state (or the fight / flight / fawn response)

When our brain gets a danger signal from one of our sensory organs, the amygdala starts pumping adrenaline, asking the brain to send more oxygen to our chest, blood to the limbs and to increase the heart rate. It is preparing the body to defend itself (to fight) or to run away from danger (flight). This is the body in active survival mode – it is getting ready to perform an action like run away or fight to defend itself. This response can be generated by several different situations, and in the case of a child it is generally activated more regularly than an adult.

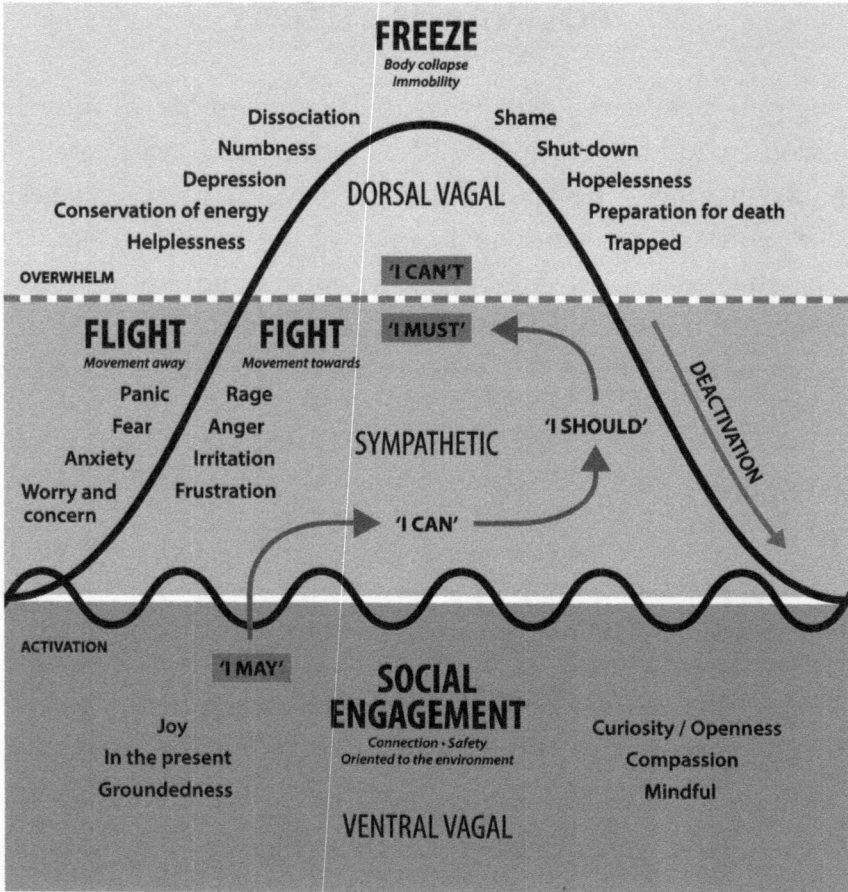

FREEZE
Body collapse
Immobility

Dissociation   Shame
Numbness   Shut-down
Depression   **DORSAL VAGAL**   Hopelessness
Conservation of energy   Preparation for death
Helplessness   Trapped

OVERWHELM   'I CAN'T'

FLIGHT **FIGHT** 'I MUST'
Movement away *Movement towards*

Panic   Rage
Fear   Anger   'I SHOULD'
Anxiety   Irritation   **SYMPATHETIC**
Worry and Frustration
concern

'I CAN'

DEACTIVATION

ACTIVATION

'I MAY'   **SOCIAL**
ENGAGEMENT
Connection · Safety
Joy   *Oriented to the environment*   Curiosity / Openness
In the present   Compassion
Groundedness   Mindful

VENTRAL VAGAL

Why? Because the child's danger response system (the amygdala) is not yet fully formed, and the hippocampus – the part of the brain that registers memory – is also not fully stocked. So the child has less opportunity to assess the situation based on experience compared to an adult. In other words, they have less data to compare it to. For example, a child may experience something as life-threatening or terrifying because it is unknown, whereas an adult with more life experience may make a more rational assessment of the danger. A child is more likely to enter a sympathetic state, and more quickly, than an adult, because of their developing brain and lack of experience. So, for example, a child may encounter struggles at school, the loss of a pet or friendship challenges as far more overwhelming than an adult, who may have built up a resilience bank of experiences related to relationships, death and failure.

The fawn response is a lesser-known trauma response, but forms in response to multiple threat experiences when the body has decided that this time it will try to 'befriend' or 'appease' the threat. This is toxic people-pleasing 101; it is a child who decides that the threat can't be run away from, fought or ignored, so you must ask the threat to go away by doing what it wants. These children do not like to show negative emotion such as sadness or anger; they turn the feelings in on themselves rather than risk the threat of directing them towards the aggressor. They will constantly monitor for signs of threat or displeasure in another, and modify their behaviour so as not to poke the danger.

Dorsal state (or the freeze response)

When danger seems completely overwhelming, and active survival (fight / flight / fawn) is no longer an option, the body will use its last survival technique: the dorsal response. Here, the body will engage a pathway in the dorsal vagal system (in the abdomen) that causes total shut-down: the heart rate drops, breathing is very slow and digestion stops or empties. The system has gone on to standby, and the body 'freezes'. We see this in animals who play dead in response to a predator, and in children in response to danger from an adult (a child cannot fight or run away from an adult so the body makes the clever decision to play dead). If the freeze response is ignored by the predator and the threat continues, the body's limbic system and vagal system short circuit and a process called dissociation happens.

DISSOCIATION

Dissociation is a key component of PTSD (post-traumatic stress disorder), and it is also a good way to differentiate between 'traumatic impact' and PTSD. We can feel traumatised by being in the sympathetic state, in other words we can have memories that remind us of feeling high anxiety, or scared, but we are not yet in the dorsal state. The dorsal state is the space where PTSD forms due to its connection to the process of dissociation and the subsequent memory disruption that occurs.

Dissociation is primarily a mental freeze and what I consider to be the body's final survival tool, when even the freeze (dorsal) state doesn't work. It happens via the shutting down of the vagal nerve and the thalamus (the memory decoder). It says: I cannot prevent this happening to my body, but I can attempt to remove the brain memory functions from this experience to stop the record button. In other words: body, we don't need to remember this.

So, while this memory short circuit is going on and the body is frozen, we go to a place where people might describe feeling 'out of their body', or 'watching themselves from above'. This seems a good survival response, but what it can't do is stop the physical trauma happening, so the physical body still feels the sensations of fear, pain or grief even if the brain is trying not to 'record' it. A flood of data has come into the brain, but it isn't 'time stamped' (the computer screen went black at the time of the memory development) and the brain doesn't know how to file these sensations. The memory system of the hippocampus is completely confused.

In order to recover from this state, the body must then deactivate backwards via the states. So, for example, from dissociation the body might go back to freeze, then to sympathetic, and finally back to ventral. This is why we might see no emotion from someone directly after a trauma, but later we may see panic attacks, crying or anger. Depending on the intensity of the trauma, the flat feeling of the dorsal state could take days to work through the body.

FIGHT / FLIGHT SYSTEM MYTH DISPELLING

I often see the words fight / flight response used incorrectly, so I want to explain why it is important to understand the biological response that happens in the brain when the response is activated. It is a chemical adrenaline flood as a survival response to a threat. In children, as we have already explained, a threat may be interpreted more loosely than in an adult, so we need to help children navigate this chemical response to help them rationalise their emotions and interpret the idea of threat in a more proportionate way.

As an example of a time I have seen this response used inaccurately, I will give you an exchange I had recently. I am a huge fitness enthusiast and I love to do high intensity interval training. Recently a good friend said to me: 'That is not good for your hormonal system as it promotes the fight / flight response – it tricks your body into it.' The conviction with which this statement was said surprised me and also prompted me to do a quick internet search of how many other people were saying this. To my surprise, it was quite a lot.

Your fight / flight response is only triggered when your sensory organs send threat information to your amygdala; categorically you cannot 'run' yourself into a state where you are activating this, as your sensory organs do not receive danger signals. You will not go to a high intensity exercise class and develop PTSD. You might be tired, but you will not be tricking your body into believing it is running for its life, particularly if you have a fully functioning adult brain, and to that end I have never seen children running around to the point of exhaustion and feeling 'triggered' by this.

As a trauma specialist, very few things annoy me more than seeing clinical trauma terminology being bandied about incorrectly. The term 'triggered', for example, is now used by social media to describe feeling irritated, and 'hypervigilance' is used for situations where someone is experiencing a mild anxiety peak. 'Dissociation' is used by mainstream media to describe a state of not concentrating, and someone recently told me that Dissociative Identity Disorder (DID) is trending on TikTok as a growing community. To put that into context, my mentor – who has worked for 40 years in high-security in-patient wards – has seen three confirmed diagnoses of DID in his entire career; I have seen none. DID is thought to be caused by extreme childhood trauma that forces the sufferer to create 'alters', or other personalities, that psychotically 'split', and exist separately from each other; it is a condition thought to affect less than 0.01 per cent of the population. But apparently this tiny minority all find themselves on TikTok, and in a coincidentally similar age bracket.

Fight / flight responses are SURVIVAL responses; they are more likely to be activated in children due to their brain being underdeveloped and their memory having a much smaller data storage system.

Something that I often like to do with my child when I am feeling triggered by anger or irritation: look down at their hand.

Take a good look at the size of their hand in comparison to yours.

Note how tiny and fragile it is.

Children are significantly smaller than an adult; we might think this is obvious but it is so important that we remember this when we consider child trauma. The physical size of a child in comparison to an adult makes an adult reaction seem potentially life threatening. An adult can appear a dangerous being to a child: never take for granted the power you have over the small beings in your life, because even if **you** don't notice . . . **they** do.

LITTLE T TRAUMA VS BIG T TRAUMA

One of the things that was important to me in writing this book was helping to clearly define what is considered by clinical definition trauma, and what is by my definition little t trauma. Trauma in clinical terms usually applies to an event such as rape, assault, war, natural disaster, severe accident or threat to life. Little t trauma could be applied to any number of incidents, but only trauma will be applicable in the case of PTSD, which is a clinical term where an individual experiences symptoms impacting memory and physical responses, and giving rise to emotional disturbances. There has been significant debate around why diagnostic manuals define the criteria of an event that causes PTSD, with the argument being anything can be 'traumatic'. Yes it can, but in order for the term PTSD to be used, the event must be considered 'likely to cause significant distress', and although there are slight differences in certain diagnostic manuals, it is rarely open to subjectivity.

The event cannot include exposure to trauma via media, and in the case of bereavement, the death must have occurred outside of 'natural causes'. There will be people who feel this is an unfairly reductive analysis of what is traumatic, but it is important that the medical community sets parameters for PTSD so they can diagnose it accurately. If any event can be defined as causing PTSD, it makes the diagnosis much more open to interpretation, and potentially to being applied incorrectly. This does NOT mean that because you don't have PTSD you have not suffered trauma, it simply means that the clinical diagnosis cannot be applied.

WHAT IS A TRIGGER?

I said earlier that I feel quite irritated when people use the term 'triggered' inaccurately. Why? Because it is the misuse of an important process. A trigger is a sensation or reminder of an event that happened to you in the past that is traumatic. It pokes the emotional part of the brain to look for a clue – where does this memory belong? When did this happen? The brain may not find the correct place for this data, in which case the body reacts seemingly irrationally or disproportionately to something, because it doesn't realise it is responding to a past trauma. The body is reliving something as if it is currently happening, because this traumatic memory, which may not have been stored and coded properly, is not being processed by the brain as past 'data'. This is particularly true for traumas that occurred when the brain was developing.

SO WE SHOULD ALL 'GET ON WITH IT' THEN?

I am not here to open a debate on why the medical community views trauma in this way. For some people it is not easy to hear that the trauma they suffered is not classed as PTSD, but when we use the term incorrectly we are potentially undermining the distress of those for whom PTSD is a crippling illness. But just because someone else doesn't define what happened to you as traumatic does not mean it did not have a traumatic impact on you.

Let's take the example of the parent with alcoholism. Now, if that parent's alcoholism also involved verbal / physical / sexual abuse then you most certainly would meet 'event trigger' criteria for PTSD, but if not then you might not. The danger of clinging on to the medical definition of trauma here is that it removes the very strong possibility that you may have endured the experience of an 'absent' parent, a parent you had to play carer to, a parent whose moods you couldn't predict, a parent who often didn't show up for things or was generally unpredictable or embarrassing. Maybe you never had friends come over or never wanted to introduce them to your parent. All of these experiences may have affected the way you view yourself and family models, and they may affect the way you parent or how you feel about becoming a parent.

Using the childhood experience of having learning difficulties as a further example, maybe you suffered from dyslexia, and when you were asked to read in front of the class felt your whole body tense up, and your voice choking. While dyslexia is not trauma, it may impact how you now feel speaking in front of others, or whether you view yourself as 'clever'. Perhaps you feel resentful of your educational experience, or maybe you still panic when presented with large amounts of written information. Dyslexia sufferers often feel triggered when asked to work to loose briefs, maybe even becoming irritable or procrastinating in order not to expose their vulnerability.

What does traumatic impact look like? It is highly common for a PTSD sufferer to experience huge memory gaps and emotional instability. But even if the trauma was not significant enough to cause PTSD, a memory of something upsetting or scary can have a similar impact, particularly in young children.

INCIDENTS THAT CAUSE TRAUMATIC IMPACT

The term Adverse Childhood Experience (ACE) was first coined in a study (Felitti: 1998) that wanted to investigate how certain life events can have a lasting traumatic impact on a child's life. So, what can be considered an ACE? This could be the loss of a parent, divorce, bullying, parental addiction, poor parental mental health, moving home / schools repeatedly, abuse, neglect and exposure to violent environments. ACEs are so important to understand as they are thought to have both physical impacts, on health, as well as psychological.

A recent study showed that the likelihood of experiencing poor educational performance and declining physical and mental health over a life-span shot up rapidly when someone experienced four or more ACEs. This statistic makes for sobering reading but goes to show just how far the shock waves of childhood trauma can reach. We will never fully prevent ACES – after all, bereavement and divorce happen – but our goal as a society should be to focus on preventing ACEs from growing in number, and on treating their impact early so that we don't see these later adverse outcomes.

IN WHAT WAYS DOES TRAUMA MANIFEST IN CHILDREN?

Pre-school-age children
- Toilet issues (not previously experienced)
- Screaming / crying more than usual
- Extreme separation anxiety
- Aggressive behaviour (especially if not previously exhibited)

School-age children
- Have a hard time concentrating at school
- Unexplained vomiting or food refusal
- Difficulty sleeping – insomnia or nightmares
- Feelings of guilt or shame connected to an event
- Anxious or fearful in a variety of situations (especially if uncommon previously)

Teens
- Self-harm
- Eating disorders
- Depression

- Beginning to abuse alcohol or drugs
- Engaging in risky sexual behaviour
- Making impulsive, dangerous decisions
- Withdrawing

This list is of course not exhaustive, and we will explore in depth some common childhood traumas such as divorce, bereavement or bullying later on in the book. But the key thing to remember here is that trauma symptoms tend to group themselves into three categories: avoiding remembering the event, negative thoughts about self or others, and negative behavioural changes.

CHAPTER 2: HOW DOES OUR OWN TRAUMA IMPACT THE WAY WE PARENT?

You may be wondering why I am putting this chapter in here when this book is about your child. Well, hopefully from the previous chapter you will have started to see how early experiences have a lasting impact on us as we develop and become parents. I say that with love and without judgement, as the last thing I would want anyone to take away from this book is that 'I have traumatic experience therefore I am a bad parent'. Categorically no; recognising you may have had experiences that have caused you traumatic impact makes you a fantastic parent! In fact, it makes you a rare parent, as I would argue we are one of the first generations of parents who actively look at our own emotional reactions before we try to control our child's.

As a trauma therapist I have been so delighted to see more and more focus in parenting media on what our experiences of being parented taught us, and how this affects our parenting choices. I would like to move that conversation on, by not only looking at the way we were parented, but how we were shown to cope with adversity, as modelled by our parents.

PUT YOUR GLOVES UP: WHAT'S YOUR FIGHTING STYLE?

I adore being a therapist, and I wouldn't change it for the world, but there is one style of therapy that I find more exhausting, more emotionally demanding and more triggering than any other . . . couples therapy. I am not unusual in this; a beloved colleague of mine who has spent most of her career working in high-security hospitals once told me: 'I don't do couples, I just find I end up agreeing with one of them and thinking that it really is all the other person's fault.' What I found so hilarious about this comment from my highly trained and highly competent colleague is that it perfectly summarises why couples therapy is so damn hard. Couples therapy contains all the juicy bits of family life – the gender roles, the scapegoating, the placation, the martyrdom, the disappointment, the rage, the love . . . you get the picture of what makes family 'systems' (see page 62) so traumatising. Watching a couple navigate life, love and taxes is one of our earliest experiences as a child, when we watch the parental figures in our lives try to work out who is doing what in this house and who is raising this child?! So, when we find ourselves now playing the role of the 'adult', what do we want to show the child?

The way we fight and the way we process conflict is absolutely key in teaching our child how to handle adversity. Knowing when to hold your ground and when to concede is a life skill, as is knowing how to express yourself honestly and compassionately to people you are intimate with.

I am not going to consume the rest of this book telling you to always argue with your partner from the 'I' place and to begin every sentence, 'When you do that, I feel X . . .' because that's not real life. In that vein I would like to share another story with you: four years ago, I was on a long-haul flight with my toddler, baby and husband. The flight was full and we had been allocated separate seats. I had both the children, and my husband took the aisle. After a tense and quietly snarling showdown about who was going to fold the buggy into the overhead, and who was going to change the first nappy, I decided to viciously whisper to David, my husband, what I thought he should go and do with himself in that moment . . . Unfortunately for me, the people sitting next to David, who heard my less than compassionate exchange, happened to be a couple . . . a couple who saw me for couples therapy. I was now confronted with the dilemma that a therapist always feels when they see their patients in the 'real world'. I could not acknowledge or say hello to them unless they approached me. They didn't; presumably they were either too shocked to hear that Dr Alison swears at her husband or they were simply as uncomfortable as I was. I apologised to David and admitted I was tired and stressed and frankly behaving like a baby; and then sat back down and spent the next 11 hours trying to be as invisible as possible so as not to break the therapist 'fourth wall' any more than I already had.

Of course, I am not advocating that you should speak to your partner in the way I did, but the reality is we all do it now and again. My children may or may not remember that exchange. I didn't swear at David in front of them and actually as a couple we have always tried to not do this – and generally we don't – but they likely will have seen two parents extremely stressed and dealing with their own feelings of resentment and exhaustion in different (and yes, unhealthy) ways. One thing I would like to think that my children always see is that we are great apologisers, and we will often stop mid-fight to acknowledge the idiots we are being and to try to pull the situation back from the brink. I hope my children will take away from this the idea that no conflict is irreparable, laughter is always a good way to stop a conflict, and apologies are important things.

Couples' conflict styles and impact on a child

All couples will adopt at least one of the following styles at different points in the relationship, but what I would like us to think about is the impact on the child for the conflict style they see **regularly** adopted in their home.

Avoidant

This style is 'agreeing to disagree', and minimising conflict where possible; it is also sometimes thought of as 'picking your battles'. While this is not obviously destructive for a child to witness, it can be insidious in the sense it teaches children that conflict is something to fear and that conflict is not easy to repair.

Volatile

A highly emotional style that will often involve passionate disagreement or debate; this is not necessarily a sign that a couple is handling conflict poorly but it can be easily misinterpreted by children as aggression. This style may be well tolerated by the couple but a child cannot tell the difference between shouting as a means of expression and shouting as a means of 'control'.

Validating

A style where one person seeks to understand the other's beliefs and empathise with them. This can feel the most stabilising to a child as it does not deny the reality of conflict but seeks to acknowledge it from an emotionally regulated place. This is the style that can teach children how to effectively express themselves in conflict, without people pleasing.

Hostile

The most damaging conflict style for a child to witness, this style may not always have the same 'drama' as the volatile style but it may be characterised by feelings of resentment or contempt. This style, if it is adopted regularly, is always destructive in nature to a relationship. Children who witness this style of conflict regularly will believe that conflict is destructive, always needs to be 'won', and that emotional abuse is acceptable when one is angry.

If you find yourself regularly engaging in hostility or competitive styles of arguing with your partner, I urge you to take stock of what you are doing and attempt to manage the causes of this contempt. Couples who have suffered relationship trauma such as infidelity, financial instability or resentful gender roles and are now operating with hostility (whether it be overt or silent) will often tell their couples therapist that they 'are great co-parents'. But choosing to parent with another person whom you feel hostility towards is categorically not great parenting, it is modelling conflict as a relationship style. Frequent and poorly resolved conflict between couples puts children at risk for mental health issues, academic problems and social issues. It teaches them to be anxious, distraught or hopeless.

Remember this: a child learns their attachment style from their primary attachment figure, but they learn their conflict style from how their parents fight each other. Teach them to fight fairly.

TELL ME ABOUT YOUR PARENTS . . .

Our parents had parents, and those grandparents had parents. We are passing down a lineage of experiences and beliefs that are both helpful and deeply unhelpful. We are re-parenting time and again by the way somebody chose to parent seven generations back from us. So what have we actually absorbed through the passage of time about what a good parent is?

I would now like to draw out some specific examples of how traumas can impact our parenting choices and styles; there are a great number of examples, and this list is of course not exhaustive, but is intended to offer drawn-out explanations of how generational trauma works, and how patterns in parenting carry on through our lineage.

The traumatised parent

For parents who might have grown up in homes where people were violent, neglectful or abusive, parenting can be a minefield. If your experience of being a child was one of chaotic boundaries, and where fear and shame were used as mind-control tactics, how can you safely set boundaries in your own family?

If you have been abused, the world has shown you that there is danger and shame everywhere and it can be hard to protect yourself from it, so you may find yourself trying to scare your child into avoiding it. You may be facing overwhelming anxiety about play dates / sleepovers or places where other adults have access to your child without you being there. You may find you want to read and consume a lot of material about identifying 'dangerous people', or talking to your child about them, in order to believe that knowledge will be power and you can save them from the cruelty you endured. Or you may feel disgust at your child's comfort in their body or sexuality and find yourself getting angry at them or attempting to humiliate them. It might be that in your home shame was used as a method of preventing a behaviour, so you are resorting to a learned tactic. These are all symptoms of unresolved trauma and I strongly advise anyone who suffers these to seek help.

What is actually going here?

When a parent has previously experienced trauma, their body holds those memories within the survival system (the limbic centre of the brain). When we become a parent, biologically we instantly incorporate this child into our own survival system – we are now responsible for not only our survival but also THEIR survival. Think back to the last safety demonstration you sat through on a plane, where they tell you to fix your own oxygen mask before fixing that of others . . . why do they do this? Because research shows that a parent will ALWAYS attempt to prioritise the survival of a child before their own; the human race is biologically programmed to continue its lineage in order to survive as a species, so we protect our young sometimes to the detriment of ourselves.

So, going back to the parent's body that holds its own trauma, when that body is triggered to be reminded of the trauma but this time in relation to their child, the body will send messages that danger is present and you must attend to this immediately: your child's survival is equal to your own. While I realise I have spent a large amount of time telling parents not to see a child as an extension of themselves and that this is narcissistic, unfortunately the survival system in our brain doesn't want to listen to this message and will always see our offspring's survival as interlinked to our own.

So in the traumatised parent, the brain senses danger related to memories from the past and it sends adrenaline flying round the body, prompting the fight or flight response. In the case of the traumatised parent, where you try to prevent the child from engaging in the activity or behaviour that is spiking your adrenaline, you are responding with the flight response. Or in the case of engaging in a fight with your child in order to get them to sense the 'danger', you are engaging your fight response. While the child themselves is not the threat to the parent, the parent's limbic system is working on overdrive and engages the child in a 'fight' in order to calm the adrenaline and neutralise the 'threat' – the behaviour that is triggering.

How can we stop parenting from a triggered state?

In this example where the trigger directly connects to a past trauma that you are aware of – and this part is key – I advise you to go to therapy to help process that trauma. Evidence-based therapies for processing previous trauma can include EMDR, trauma-focused CBT or Narrative Exposure Therapy. However, more often than not, the parent is not actually aware that this does connect to a previous trauma, and they cannot articulate why this behaviour is causing them so much distress, so let's now look at some of those examples.

The 'everything was fine' childhoods

How was your childhood? Yeah, pretty fine actually . . . Far more often than not, this is the response I hear to the above question from adults who have come to talk to me. People who did not grow up in homes where there was obvious domestic violence or abuse often feel that the right answer to the question is, 'yeah, it was fine'. I call this the 'starving children' phenomenon, where parents of previous generations would often berate a child for not finishing their meal with the words, 'There are children in this world . . .' In other words, everyone else has it harder than you so why complain. While I get the previous generation's attempts at promoting resilience, and also, frankly, an easier mealtime, this parenting technique has raised a later generation of parents who don't feel comfortable acknowledging that their own experience of being parented was frankly not that fine.

Parents who grew up in homes with 'anger issues'

Maybe you grew up in a home where discipline was frequent and punishments were harsh. Maybe people shouted a lot or you were punished for minor infringements.

Maybe you were often humiliated or belittled by family members. If you are one of these people, as a parent you might find it challenging to engage with children when they are testing boundaries, and you might find that you respond either over-punitively or you attempt to placate them.

Boundaries and the importance of them is often touted as the reason for upholding harsh discipline, but the problem with this is that it is not teaching boundaries at all – it is teaching the subjugation of another via controlling or threatening behaviour. A parent who has grown up in a home like this who is now parenting another may struggle to set boundaries with their child; they may wish to become overly lenient, in order to maintain 'happiness' and 'a quiet life', or they may feel enraged at the challenge the child is posing to their perceived authority, and lash out.

What is actually going on here?

When something your child does pushes your boundaries or throws you into conflict, you may immediately go into a state of high cortisol (the stress hormone). The reason for this is that in your home growing up, conflicts weren't dealt with in a kind way, and healthy anger was not displayed; conflict was a battleground and there was a victor and a victim. Arguments were a survival scenario where one person would succeed and another would lose. So now as a parent you find yourself not knowing how to handle the conflict with your own child without feeling that dysregulated, pumping adrenaline state of 'this is a fight'.

You may also have been taught to believe that anger is an emotion that we should all fear. It may or may not surprise you to learn that the emotion I have yet to see ANY adult patient of mine have a healthy relationship with is anger. Previous generations of parents taught us that anger is something to be avoided as anger = aggression. Anger created arguments, anger was something that showed a lack of discipline or control, anger resulted in physical punishment, anger was 'uncouth'. Any of these messages promotes the idea in us as adults that we must fear the natural anger of our child and we must do everything in our power to contain it and control it. In parents who have had experiences of anger being used as a tool to humiliate or control, we may now choose to 'meet fire with fire' when dealing with our child's anger in order to control them. You may do anything in your power to not let them get angry, as in your experience when someone is angry with you it is a disastrous thing.

What are we going to do about this thing, 'anger'?

If you are choosing to always avoid disciplining your child for fear of evoking their anger, or you are controlling your child for fear of authority challenges, you need to consider the body state you are coming from. A little bit of adrenaline is fine when we feel conflict – that is normal – but to fear that anger will cause an adrenaline so huge that we will become uncontrolled suggests a major issue with the emotion of anger. I would encourage you to reflect back on how conflicts were handled in your home: re-read the couples' arguing styles on page 30 and think about how your parents did it? Consider your own relationship with anger and ask yourself these three questions the next time you feel anger rising in your role as a parent:

- Are my expectations reasonable?
- Am I truly understanding the other person's perspective?
- Do I have the power to really change this situation?

Anger is so often about our own fear of being out of control; we were told that anger was a dangerous emotion and we might have been shown by our parents that anger results in aggression. When we can release a little bit of our need to control, and we can allow ourselves the space to feel the fear – 'I am not entirely in control here' – we can actually step back and recognise the three key things for keeping anger 'healthy'.

- The facts: what is actually going on here?
- The proportions: is my response proportional to the 'offence'?
- The impact: how much can I change and how much does it actually matter if I don't?

FINANCIAL / HOUSING CHAOS: MASLOW'S HIERARCHY OF NEEDS

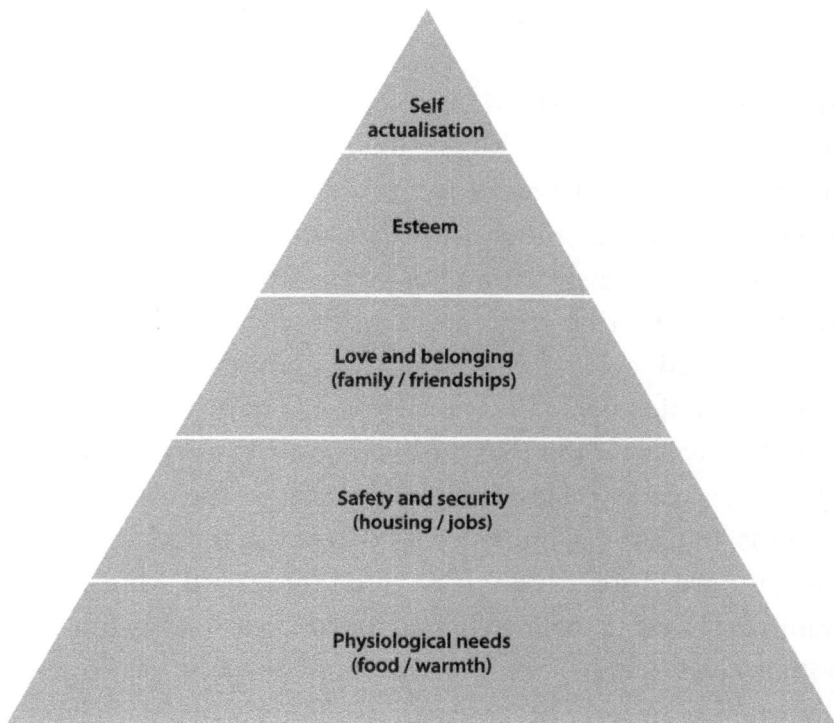

American psychologist Abraham Maslow wrote a famous paper in 1943 called 'The Hierarchy of Needs', and at the bottom of the pyramid before we get close to love and belonging, he put two chunky bases: physiological needs (food / warmth / clean air) and then just above that safety and security (money / housing etc.). For many families, these two base layers of needs are the primary drivers of their everyday life; they fight on a daily basis to simply put food on the table and a roof over everyone's head.

Maybe your parents had a number of financial challenges

that meant there was often a lot of chaos around logistics in the home and you felt that nothing was ever easy; people worked many jobs, and there were a lot of arguments about money or housing. From a young age you were aware that things were tight or that certain aspects of life such as money or jobs caused your parents a lot of stress, so in order to be a good child you didn't want to add to their stress. You decided to stick to focusing on these two base layers of the pyramid rather than demand people's time and attention with your emotional needs.

It can be extremely painful for people from these households to acknowledge that the trauma of financial instability their parents faced every day meant that they could not always provide emotionally in the way they would have liked. It can feel like a betrayal to admit that the mum you saw working two jobs sometimes made you feel less important than the task of paying the bills. In these instances, I would urge you to remember that we can have absolute compassion for the parent who suffered trauma, while still feeling compassion for our own feelings. We do not need to create a narrative where a parent who suffered the strain of poverty or financial instability is marked as a 'bad parent'; that would be cruel and entirely inaccurate, as we will see in the next example. Financial resources do not guarantee good parenting, but we can acknowledge that these environmental challenges, maybe through no fault of your parents, created trauma.

AFFLUENT NEGLECT

My career has taken me to many places and I have worked with many different types of parents, but let's now get into what I would consider the most under-documented form of neglect: affluent neglect. Throughout my time in private practice, I have seen far more of this type of neglect than any other.

This is a home where money was not lacking, material goods of all kinds were always available, holidays and extracurricular activities abounded. You had 'model' parents. If you grew up in this home, from the outside there were definitely people who had it 'worse' than you, but maybe outside of all this box ticking of the 2.4 family model, you felt something lacked. Maybe your parents had high-pressure jobs and often didn't have time for you; maybe you were often placated with toys or treats rather than true attention; maybe 'childish' interests seemed less important than the 'adult' activities.

Maybe you felt that in all this outward display of achievement, you also had to achieve; grades were a big issue and you felt you had to achieve things that would make your parents proud in order to gain their love. Maybe you also felt that your job as a child was to win the love of your parents by doing good and impressive things; you knew instinctively that they responded positively when you had done something worthy of attention, and you always fought hard to do this. You liked to push yourself academically or in your extracurricular activities in the hope that they would answer the question, 'Now will you love me?' with a big resounding yes.

Perhaps you never really felt you met their standards or lived up to their high expectations; they often reminded you how many sacrifices they had made to get you here and you had 'failed' them in some way. Maybe you have always lived your adult life with the feeling that you need to do more, or that you haven't quite done enough. You have been taught that love is something that one must win, and love is shown in outward displays of things and actions, rather than as an unconditional feeling.

What is going on here with all this emotional neglect?

All of these different experiences of emotional neglect can have subtle but pernicious impacts on your parenting. You may find it hard to connect with your own child, as affection was not something you were used to as a child; you may find your child's need for emotional intimacy cloying, tiring or annoying. You may also feel uncomfortable with expressing physical affection or telling your children you love them. You may even find that you long for your child to get older, and for them to become more independent and less dependent on you. This might be because you did not experience a parent relationship where you could rely on them to protect you or care for you, and now you find it strange to have to do it for someone else.

Adults who were emotionally neglected are far more likely to reject or reduce the emotions of others; they have an almost pathological fear of emotion. The belief is if someone shows large amounts of sadness or anger, then 'I may not be able to control it and this is a bad thing'. Emotionally neglected parents may fear that they cannot stop their child's tears and they hurry to placate them or scold them for crying. They rarely do this consciously, but their unconscious reaction when they see their child becoming frustrated or angry is to end the situation. Let's look at an example:

Scenario: Child whines and cries when leaving the playground

Parent A (the panic tactic): 'I'm going . . . OK, bye then, OK, bye then . . . I'm leaving . . . come on, you don't want to be left behind' (parent walks towards the gate of the playground until the child follows).

Parent B (the distraction tactic): 'It's OK, look what Mummy has, I have a snack for you / do you want to look at Mummy's phone in the buggy?'

Parent C (the bribing tactic): 'If you come now, I'll buy you a treat in the supermarket.'

Parent D (the discipline tactic): 'I'm not having this. I've said no, we are leaving now' (manhandling the child out of the playground and into the buggy).

Parent E (the smothering tactic): 'Shhh . . . shhh . . . shhh . . . please don't cry, oh no, it's OK . . . shhh shhh, I know, I know' (parent cuddles child but does not engage with them, parent appears panicked).

Which of these parenting tactics is a possible sign of an underlying fear of 'big emotion'?

All of them.

Every single of one of these examples I have done personally, and none of them are intrinsically bad or wrong, but what they are all doing in different ways is shutting down the emotion. They are actively backing away from the child's anger and frustration; none of them are choosing to engage in the reality that the child feels angry at this point. Parent E's tactic is one I see with a lot of parents who have children who tantrum a lot, and while it appears the most empathetic what it actually does is rejects the core emotion of frustration by attempting to smother it.

How to comfort a crying child: the box of tissues example

Parent E's reaction reminds me of something that happened to me as a trainee therapist. I was being observed giving a 'therapy session' to my fellow trainee who had begun to cry. I had decided to reach over and place the box of tissues closer to her, and I wrapped up the assessment feeling very pleased with myself about how closely I had followed the formulation we were supposed to be demonstrating, and generally what a good therapist I had been. That is until the following exchange with my tutor:

> *One question, Alison: the tissues, why did you pass them?*
> Because they were crying . . .
> *Could they reach them themselves?*
> Yes, but I wanted to show them I was coming alongside them (forgive the earnest trainee therapy-speak 'coming alongside' a patient, but many moons ago I did tend to fall back on such therapy-speak clichés. I am sure if any of my current clients read this, the thought of me using that phrase now will give them a good laugh . . .).
> *OK, so in order to do that, to 'come alongside' them, you wanted them to stop crying?*
> Er no . . . (I was really floundering now, wondering what on earth I had done wrong).
> *But a tissue is often passed because we want someone to wipe their tears away, no?*
> I didn't mean it like that.
> *How often do you see people who, after being passed a tissue, stop crying?*

I have thought about this exchange many times, and actually

if you ask any therapist they will tell you that the placement of the box of tissues in the room is often very strategic. General rule of thumb is to place it within reach but to not proffer it: why? Because pushing the box of tissues towards the clients unconsciously communicates: 'I would like you to be spared the indignity of crying, here, clean yourself up.' Obviously in therapy everything is contextualised, and I have had some clients for whom the offering of a tissue would be well received and this would not feel like shutting them down, and I have had some for whom to be able to ugly cry is a wonderful release of previous trauma. But if even therapists carry the unconscious bias of tears = bad, what are parents supposed to do?

Everyone wants to comfort their crying child and this can be a wonderfully connecting, attachment securing moment, or it can be stifling. The key here is the message that the comforting contains. I would encourage you to cuddle / console and simply say:

Let it out, I am not going anywhere.

In this simple sentence we remind the child of three important things:

- Your big emotions don't scare me
- You are loved
- All of you is welcome here

So the next time we find ourselves triggered by our child's tears of anger or sadness, rather than reacting to internal messaging we received as children – that emotions are a sign of weakness or are dangerous – allow them their space. Welcome them in and let them breathe; when we do this we are not only healing our own traumatic messages, we are ensuring that our child does not carry the same damaging ideas of 'only the comfortable parts of you are allowed in here'.

Identifying YOUR own parenting triggers

Even if the none of the above parenting traumas fit you or your lived experience, it's highly likely that you have endured difficult memories from your own upbringing, and you have given some thought to how you might avoid repeating the same patterns with your child. The primary advice I would give is to begin to understand your own triggers – so how do we do this?

A key pointer I give to parents to acknowledge their triggers is: when do they feel they have parented in a way they have later regretted? For example, when did they notice that they reacted more sharply or aggressively than they would have liked? Or when did they feel 'stuck' in response to their child's behaviour or action? These triggers often connect to what psychology terms 'core beliefs', which are beliefs that someone told you about yourself or others that you have internalised as an irrefutable truth. Sadly, core beliefs can often be negative, and part of going to therapy can be the dissecting of these negative core beliefs and replacing them with healthier ones.

The answers to these questions may look very different, but here are some real-life examples of triggers I have helped parents acknowledge, and their corresponding core beliefs:

- Feeling rage when smacked by toddler. (I am the adult and my child MUST respect me.)
- Feeling on edge about a child who is displaying poor

table manners. (My child's behaviour is a reflection on me.)

- Wanting to leave the room when faced with a tantrum. (I am scared of anger because it is 'uncontrollable'.)
- Feeling stumped by a teenager's verbal outburst. (When people shout at me it means they don't love me.)
- Feeling rage at a teenager's defiance. (Children should obey a parent.)
- Becoming easily angered when travelling on a plane or eating in a restaurant with a child for fear of others' opinion of child's behaviour. (Other people judge me negatively.)
- Feeling shame for child's public tantrum. (People will think I cannot control my child, and that is a parent's job.)
- Feeling panicked by child's sexual development. (Sex is shameful.)
- Feeling angered by toilet 'accidents'. (You are deliberately trying to anger me.)
- Feeling silenced by a child's aggression. (I am scared by anger; it destroys things.)
- Feeling shame for having a child who is not 'clever', 'beautiful', 'popular'. (I am scared of being a 'failure'.)

Examples of healthier cognitions that I have worked with to combat the above negative core beliefs might be as follows:

- I do not have to parent for the approval of others. I trust my judgement.
- I don't have to take things personally.
- I am loved and respected by my children.

- I do not have to meet anger with aggression, I am in control of me.
- I am the perfect parent for my child.
- Children aren't perfect, but neither am I.
- You don't have to be a perfect parent, just a loving one.
- Every day I am trying my best, and every day I am getting better.
- I am a kind and compassionate parent.
- I trust my children and they trust me.
- I do not own my children, but I am blessed to have them in my life.

This book is about your child, but what I hope this chapter has shown you is that above all parenting is not something that is done to your child, it is something that HAPPENS between parent and child. It is a dynamic, rather than a static, action. You were also parented, you bring in all of those experiences and core beliefs into your parenting, and it's highly possible that those core beliefs go back generations. So how do we distil all of this into something digestible?

- Identify your own triggers; look at the suggested examples and consider if any of these are you. What is a time when you have parented in a way that made you feel stuck or ashamed? Look more deeply at what it is that YOU (not your child!) are telling yourself internally to make you feel this way.
- Get to know your lineage. What patterns have been passed down your family tree? Consider birth order and cultural understandings of parenting. What were you told about parenting from the parents that came before you?

- If we want to help our children regulate their emotions, DON'T encourage them to shut them down or be afraid of them. Allow them to express the big feelings like anger, shame and sadness, even when it feels difficult to do it.
- Children learn how to manage conflict from US, and given that anger is often considered to be one of the most difficult emotions to hold and process in a healthy way, try to model healthy forms of conflict in your home.
- We have all had different parents; if your parent was narcissistic, then do as much research as you can on the impact of narcissistic parenting. It is the most common form of parental abuse that I see among my adult survivors of child abuse.
- Scapegoating is one of the key components of narcissistic parenting and it comes in many forms: the scapegoat is not necessarily the rebel, they might also be the people pleaser. Scapegoating occurs in many families, even those where the parent is not overtly narcissistic. Parenting can evoke SOME degree of narcissism in a lot of people; get to understand what scapegoating is and how it might have played out in your family.
- Families work as a 'system' (more on this in the following chapter): there are ever-changing parts and alliances forming. In order to survive, the system often finds things or people to put all of its anxieties and fears about survival into. If the system finds a person to identify as the problem, this individual is often the most intrinsically empathetic but outwardly destructive. There's a phrase in family therapy that 'the one everyone comes to therapy about is least likely to be the problem'.

- Environmental chaos, such as poverty or housing instability, can cause trauma and there is no shame or disloyalty in acknowledging that being parented by a parent who was under environmental stress was stressful.
- Ask yourself these questions:

  ○ What would you choose to change about the way you were parented?
  ○ What would your partner choose to change about the way they were parented?
  ○ How are finances decided in your house?
  ○ How is conflict handled in your house?
  ○ What is the expectation of 'success' for your children?
  ○ How realistic is this expectation?

CHAPTER 3: ATTACHMENT

Attachment theory is one of the cornerstones of child psychology. It suggests that a child's interaction with their primary caregiver will provide a blueprint for how they view themselves in relation to others. The four attachment styles that we have come to know were developed by researchers John Bowlby and Mary Ainsworth in the 1960s and '70s. Attachment wounds, or injuries as they are sometimes called, often fall into the little t traumas categories, as they are traumas that affect someone on an interpersonal level rather than as a threat to life. Examples of attachment wounds might be divorce, bereavement, parental illness (mental and physical) or significant experiences of sibling rivalry / favouritism.

Attachment theory suggests that when a child had a caregiver who was attentive to their needs and predictable, they would experience the world as safe and manageable. When a caregiver was more distant or often unable to respond, the child might become more self-reliant – believing the world 'doesn't care'

– and untrusting of others. A caregiver whose attention was unpredictable or erratic might create a child who likes to people please or is highly anxious. The later addition of disorganised attachment was suggested to occur in abusive or frightening homes where a child has no sense of predictability or safety and must respond to the world using their biological fight / flight / fawn / freeze response.

WHAT IS YOUR ATTACHMENT STYLE?

Attachment styles are part of a theory, and I want to stress that even if you fall into one of the categories of 'insecure' attachment, that firstly you are not alone, as 35–40 per cent of the population are with you; and secondly, you can change your attachment style. You can develop secure, boundaried, loving relationships regardless of what your first experiences were. While we know that attachment theory research shows that 100 per cent of your initial attachment pattern is formed by the age of two, Davila et al. (1997) showed that a person's adaptability to change and increased emotional resilience actually improved an attachment pattern from an insecure one to a secure one in a study of 155 women assessed over three years. Likewise, Kirkpatrick and Hazan (1994), in their longitudinal study of attachment over the lifespan, showed that 30 per cent of respondents who originally had an insecure attachment pattern changed to a secure one. An attachment style is not a life sentence, but the first step to changing it is to first understand it.

Adult attachment theory exercise

In this exercise we will look at what your attachment style might be and then later on in the book we will explore how that might play into your parenting style. So, either by thinking about these in your head or writing them down, go ahead and answer these questions:

1. What phrases or adjectives come to mind when you think of your earliest memories?
2. Which parent did you feel closest to? And why do you think that was?
3. When you were upset as a child, what would you do? Who would you go to?
4. Can you describe your first memory of separation from your parents?
5. Did you ever feel rejected as a child?
6. Did your parents ever threaten you?
7. How do you think your early experiences may have affected you in adulthood?
8. Why do you think your parents behaved as they did?

Did any of the answers surprise you? Did anything come up for you as you were considering your early experiences that you wanted to reject or avoid remembering? Did you find yourself feeling anger or shame towards any of these experiences? I encourage you to be kind and compassionate to yourself as you do this work, as for those for whom home was not a safe place, this may uncover some difficult memories. I encourage you to work through these at your own pace or skip these exercises if they feel overwhelming or triggering.

Attachment patterns breakdown

Attachment forms the basis of almost every psychological theory that assesses a child's relationship with their parent, and so much has been written about it already that I am not going to consume this book with a deep dive into the various different ways this theory has been applied and researched. But it would be fair to say that it remains one of the most seminal theories of psychology, even 70 years after it was first suggested.

So what are attachment patterns and how do they play out in relationships?

Secure Attachment

This is thought to be the attachment style of 30 per cent of the global population and represents people who grew up as infants believing that their caregiver was predictable, safe and reliable. The caregiver was warm, nurturing and attentive, but NOT smothering – and this is a key differentiator. This attachment pattern has allowed the child to develop their independence. Rather than being seen as an extension of the parent, the child has been loved for who they are rather than what they can do, and the child feels confident in their own instincts and judgement.

Securely attached adults enjoy emotional intimacy with their chosen partner and feel comfortable relying on others and being relied upon. As parents they respond instinctively to their child's needs and feel comfortable in the idea of sharing a deep emotional connection with another. This does not mean these parents always have the answers or are 'perfect' parents (no perfect parent exists!) but they do not fear the emotional rollercoaster of parenting, and they try to adapt to challenges that the parenting journey throws them, without deep fear of abandonment or emotional destruction.

Securely attached parents view their child as their own being, and they try to parent them from a place where they can provide safety and security while championing the child's growing independence. They do not fear conflict and they do not fear big emotions. Again – this does not mean they deal with all conflict perfectly! But the crucial difference here is they do not view big emotions as potentially destructive to a relationship; they view it as simply what it is – a conflict. They also do not fear the emotional dependence of their child upon them, but they also do not cling to this emotional dependence for fear of being abandoned one day; they are comfortable in the unknown in relationships and are not easily triggered by ebbs and flows of emotional conflict.

Anxious Attachment (sometimes called Ambivalent)

This is an attachment style where a caregiver is unpredictable or changeable, so one minute they are loving – possibly to the point of smothering – and another minute they are absent or cold. This may sound quite extreme but this is a highly common parenting style particularly in our digital age of parental stress and large amounts of environmental stimulus vying for parents' attention. Parents now regularly work much longer hours away from home, and they have to respond to emails and messages outside of these hours. We may also see this in non-working parents who consume their life with the drive for the perfect home and family that they see on social media. The child may then interpret this parent as being unpredictable in their presence, as the parent's focus is regularly fragmented or divided.

A child who experiences this attachment believes that love is conditional. They believe it comes when you please others, and when it comes it might even be overwhelming. In fact, it might make you slightly uncomfortable, almost as though it wants to consume you. But then it is gone, and when it returns it might look different – distracted, or slightly annoyed. For now let's imagine that an anxiously attached adult will be one who feels criticised on all angles. They fear abandonment and fight to avoid it at all costs. This fight might become overwhelming and they need to withdraw.

The anxiously attached mother may fear her child's independence and fight to keep them as a child. She feels large amounts of judgement from others and often feels misunderstood and misrepresented; she feels unconfident in her gut instincts and wary of others criticising her.

Avoidant Attachment

This is an attachment style that is very common in high-achieving adults who tend to have a positive view of themselves and a negative one of others. They view relationships as unnecessary to their own happiness, and they crave independence in all things. They fear commitment, believing the other person is ultimately trying to control them, and where possible they will carve out their own mental escape routes, at times even actively destroying relationships that they believe to be overly close.

This attachment pattern is developed by an absent or inattentive parent who has taught the child that nobody is there for their emotional needs. These children become excellent self-soothers. Some research suggests that overly stringent cry-it-out techniques for sleep training can promote this attachment pattern, but equally this attachment pattern can be found in cultures around the world where such a technique has never been heard of. The key driver here is a parent who is fundamentally unreliable or emotionally unavailable. Sadly, unavoidable environmental factors such as financial instability and demanding work needs can promote this.

It can also be as a result of parental poor health or addiction and we will also explore later in the book how we can process these types of traumas and the attachment patterns they create, crucially without judgement. Parent ill health happens and so does addiction – the knock-on effect might be this attachment pattern but we will come to understand how we can compassionately acknowledge this and, crucially, how we can mitigate these issues.

Disorganised Attachment

Thankfully this is the rarest form of attachment as it is primarily created by abusive or neglectful homes. A child who has a disorganised attachment pattern grows up in a home where their fight / flight response has been constantly triggered, and as a result they suffer the poor brain development that we discussed in the previous chapter where we looked at the MRIs of chronically traumatised children. The child's trust in others will be minimal or poorly judged, they will have little to no understanding of healthy boundaries and, tragically, they are more prone than any other attachment style to developing later mental health problems, academic concerns due to the cognitive damage of chronic trauma, and addictive behaviours. These addictive behaviours may also manifest in thrill seeking or dangerous behaviour; this is down to the brain's damaged prefrontal cortex (the impulse control centre) and under-developed amygdala (the empathy centre).

This child will be emotionally volatile, they will fear others leaving but they will reject attachment with others. They will have poor self-esteem and they will not feel a sense of belonging in a family-style setting. As adults they will struggle with friendships and intimate relationships, they will also find societal boundaries such as in school and workplaces, and even legal ones, hard to follow as no one has taught them that boundaries are there to maintain safety. They fear their own boundaries being violated and as a result may violate the boundaries of others.

This type of attachment style is rare, and while it has the worst mental health prognosis, it is not a life sentence. I have personally treated many adults and children with this attachment style who have gone on to become securely attached partners and parents. The key to healing this type of attachment wound is to acknowledge it and to seek professional guidance on how to recognise and navigate the symptoms of it. This attachment pattern does not have to predict your future relationships or mental health. In order to heal from this type of attachment, you will need to show your experiences the compassion, reverence and respect they deserve. A mental health professional can help you to see how this attachment style and these early experiences have impacted you, and how you can minimise them.

Where's Dad / Gran / Aunty / adopted parent / step-parent in all of this?

Bowlby said attachment relationship came from the 'primary caregiver', but what is often ignored by parenting literature is the fact that Bowlby and more modern attachment researchers all agree that 'secondary attachment' can be AS important as the primary.

Primary doesn't mean 'better', and actually a child with more than one attachment figure is likely to be more resilient than a child with only one. Why do I make this point? Because I think this is ignored and misinterpreted in parenting mainstream literature so often. Time and again I see attachment theory being misinterpreted, forcing mothers into a space where their own needs do not exist and the idea of allowing alternative attachment figures to play a central role is experienced as 'letting the side down'. This is not only harmful to children but also to parents. Should we really, in the 21st century, be suggesting that a father is less important than a mother?

Science loves to scare us with attachment statistics. A few recent studies I read stated that children in foster care were twice as likely as war veterans to have PTSD, and another stated adoptees were four times more likely to attempt suicide than non-adoptees. As I read these statistics, I thought of the adoptive parents who must feel such distress to imagine the child they love beyond measure has a trauma stamp in their memory that they cannot erase. But I want to offer a loving arm to them to say, yes you might have some healing to do for your child, but by no means is your child destined for failure. Biology does not make a parent, and attachment is built through empathy, not biology. Promoting the idea that the biological mother is the only important relationship in child development is not helpful, and in the case of trauma, it works against a cornerstone of emotional resilience through high 'relational wealth' (i.e. lots of people who care about you).

I would like to see us take a stand and start saying that **all** early childhood attachments are what is important, not just the mother. According to psychological research a child who has this relational wealth, in other words lots of positive attachments, is more likely to develop greater emotional resilience. Children who are raised with many loving caregivers (aunts, uncles, friends, grandparents) learn that the world is a place of abundance and love, and as a result they are more likely to internalise the belief: 'I am lovable'.

THE NARCISSISM OF PARENTING

When we champion a mother relationship without acknow-ledging other attachment figures, motherhood sells you a lie: that you are the ultimate caretaker of your child's life and not the observer. This is possibly the most insidious message we are given as parents, that you have CONTROL. It just isn't true.

Love does not mean consuming and controlling another. I say this as I see mothers tortured with the realisation that all this advice stating 'just do this and you / your child will achieve X' is not true and leaves us feeling like a failure.

Your child is a blissful being of their own; you do not own them and you don't get a second go at life through them. We have the privilege of a lifetime to witness the blossoming of a tiny human into glorious adulthood. We get to observe, to listen, to celebrate the triumphs and support the losses. We get to see a life in all its acts, and we get the best seat in the house. The stage is not ours, we don't write the script and we don't direct the action – we are a loving audience member. There is nothing more narcissistic than viewing another life as being an extension of yourself; this is not good mothering, it is deeply damaging.

When children are viewed as reflections of the success of the parenting style that raised them, we are removing the entire reality that the child is their own being. I saw a programme on TV a few years ago where parents were competing to be 'Britain's best parent', and I put my head in my hands, thinking how disturbing it was that these people were all sitting around lauding their own parenting attempts, competing with others' attempts. At no point did anyone ask the ultimate decider of a parent's kindness, attentiveness or empathy: the child.

Every parent has had narcissistic moments where we have made the parenting about 'our stuff'. I managed this within myself when my eldest daughter was learning to read. She was being home schooled due to the pandemic and I was struggling a lot with what I interpreted as her 'struggle' with phonics. I found myself saying to her in panicked tones: 'Everybody learns at a different stage, it's OK.' She seemed to be surprised by this, because what she heard in my words was comfort, but my face evidently conveyed the ego wobble I was having inside, and to my shame, I believe she may have interpreted this as, 'maybe reading is a way to make Mummy happy'.

To my further shame, she would have been right. I have been academic my whole life and I was a voracious and early reader – I didn't imagine having a child who wouldn't be the same. Thankfully I realised this situation was entirely now about 'me' and nothing to do with her reading *Chip and Biff Going to the Park*.

As parents we are always learning, growing and being tested in ways we didn't know existed. By improving our awareness and becoming emotionally healthy (which let's be honest takes constant maintenance) we can become aware of how our actions can both empower and discourage our children.

THE FAMILY SYSTEM

Before we get into different types of family traumas and family models, I would like to expand on the idea of the family as a 'system', as this is absolutely key to understanding the models and dynamics that create 'family'. The founding theorist of Family Systems Theory, Murray Bowen, proposed that all humans are governed by two needs: the need for togetherness, and the need for separateness. In other words, we want to be individual but we want to have social relationships. Bowen suggested when these two needs were threatened, anxiety is provoked. So if someone in a couple feels one is pulling away, the other may respond anxiously and, depending on attachment styles, the anxious party may reject the other one or attempt to come closer to them.

The Drama Triangle

In family theory there is the belief that humans are drawn into triangles. Why? Because, considering that the shape of a triangle has two points at the base and one at the apex, the two people at the bottom gather strength by excluding the one at the top. Now, here it gets complex as the triangle doesn't always have to be three people, the third 'person' can be an addiction, a hobby or an outside interest. But what this process is always trying to do is triangulate relationships whereby two 'things' sit at the base and form an alliance, and the third person / thing can be excluded or weakened.

Now let's have a think about why we as humans might want to do that. The obvious example is the couple who decided to salvage their marital discord by having a baby. Rather than focusing on the issue of marriage we can all look at the child; both parties might now think this child is a reasonable contender to become 'supporter' within the marital conflict, and they compete for the attention of that child. Or, more commonly, they project all the stress and anxiety they have on to that child. The unconscious, in essence, finds a free bucket into which it can pour all this stuff and not have to deal with the original conflict.

So in this scenario we might see a parent who has trauma from their childhood about academic pressure pour all of this on to the child; the child is told that academic achievement is an expectation. The other parent may feel resentful about this – it reminds them of their mother-in-law whom they have never liked as she has always been dismissive of them, and they react poorly to this. They attempt to join up with the child and gang up on the 'pushy' parent. The pushy parent responds by belittling the non-pushy parent as the lenient parent and attempts to align with the child by announcing they 'only have their best interests at heart'; and so the dance goes on.

We might also see a triangle where there is marital discord due to infertility and one party's work becomes part of a triangle. The couple don't want to look at the trauma of the infertility, or the resentment one may feel towards the other around the cost of treatment, or the cause of the infertility, so work becomes the target of conflict. One person tries to engross themselves in work and the other directs all their attention and anger to combating this; they create arguments about the job and they focus on it. The job can become the 'enemy' to one and the 'saviour' to another.

Drawing the Genogram

I would like you to draw your genogram, or family diagram. There are very complicated ways to do this but we will begin by doing a basic one. I would like you to represent yourself with one shape and your partner with another; we will use circles for females and squares for male, and in the middle of them to record your ages. Also record any children you have and their ages, as in the example below.

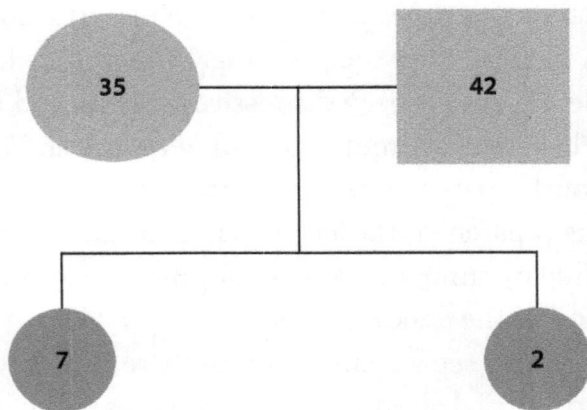

After you have done this, add your parents, and your partner's parents, and any children they had, then your grandparents and, if you know them, your great-grandparents.

Now here is where it gets revealing: I would like you to record the significant details of each of these families on this genogram, including:

- Pregnancies
- Divorces / previous partners and their children
- Known mental health issues

- Physical health issues
- Addiction issues
- Known traumas
- Abuse (including emotional, physical, sexual, financial, and neglect)

I would then like you to simply observe the genogram. What pops out to you and why? Is there any pattern that is emerging on one side of the family, are there any personality traits that appear to be prevalent through certain family lines? Note the birth order of siblings and the relationship with parents, and consider how this might have impacted them in later life. What has been passed down through your family line and finds itself being played out within your current home? Is there something that you deliberately try to avoid occurring in your current home as you can see the pattern of previous generations? What have the previous generations in your family taught you about being a parent?

On the first look this activity can maybe only bring up superficial observations such as 'there has been a history of divorce in my family', or 'there has been a history of addiction in my partner's family'. But I really want you to start thinking about the relationships that are being shown on this diagram – what kind of mother were they? What was their relationship like with their siblings? What traumas do you know they suffered? I want you to really start to dig deep into what messages you carry in your blood line about what a 'good' mother / father looks like.

I would also like us to consider the parents in that genogram who have maybe been not-so-good mothers or fathers – what did their parenting style do to the generation below them?

Doing this work, and asking ourselves these questions, helps us to see our place in the family and how the generations before us have shaped the way we parent now.

CHAPTER 4: PROMOTING RESILIENCE IN YOUR CHILD NO MATTER THE STARTING POINT

All school-aged children are faced at some point with the difficult, and possibly frightening, experience of the playground. Very quickly they have to learn things like social hierarchy, individual vs group games, and setting personal boundaries around space and attention. Most of all they have to learn how they will fit in this landscape and how they will get their needs met. Some children will do this through controlling methods towards others – giving strict instructions for their games, selecting carefully who is 'allowed' to play and who is not, maybe even isolating others.

In some cases, they might even resort to behaviour often categorised as bullying. This is of course undesirable and likely not encouraged by the adults around, but as anyone who interacts with school-aged children regularly will tell you, it happens regardless. So how can we help children express their needs in a kind, confident manner, and also manage the disappointment that comes about when this does not happen? Lastly, how can we encourage children to recognise that some children just 'don't play very nicely'?

Accepting the difficult realities of life is something almost every one of my adult patients struggles with, as do therapists. We are simply not programmed to want anything other than the best possible outcome for ourselves, so others often frustrate, anger or irritate us when this doesn't happen. In some cases this might even promote feelings of betrayal, loss or rejection. Children don't deal with these feelings any better than adults, and it's helpful for parents to remember that. Everybody can probably recall a time in the playground where someone did or said something that caused them embarrassment, hurt or anger, and the reason we hold on to those memories all those years later is that those feelings were very big and very real at the time.

In the next few pages, we will begin to explore how our children develop empathy and resilience, and how we can support the process.

HELPFUL CONVERSATION PROMPTS TO HELP YOUR CHILD DEVELOP EMPATHY

Aged 2–4

At this age children are still discovering that other people have wants and desires that may be different to their own; they operate very much in a 'just me' state – in other words, 'everything is just about me'. We often try to force children at this age to share and think about others, when biologically their brain is not yet developed enough to do this. So we find ourselves in the pattern of just repeating 'no', or 'take turns / share', to no effect and getting annoyed with the end result. Rather than doing this, focus on the concept of feelings.

At this age children will NOT fully understand the concept of empathy or being a 'nice friend'. They only just grasp that other people have a thing called feelings. We can help younger children by labelling feelings that connect directly to facial expressions:

> *Oh look, the hippo is smiling – maybe he is happy?*
> *Oh that's a grumpy face – maybe you feel angry?*

Now start labelling your feelings and connect them to an event to start to explain cause and effect:

> *When that lady offered to help me with our buggy today, I felt very happy. I was feeling tired and she helped me.*
> *I felt cross with myself that I forgot the keys, as then I had to go back to the house to get them.*

I felt sad that we didn't get to go to the park today because it was raining.

As the child gets older you can start making small connections to their behaviour and your emotions:

I felt cross when you hit me because that hurt.
I shouted because you weren't listening to me and I felt angry.

We do not overwhelm them with this connection at this stage of emotional learning as it can be very confusing for a child to realise their actions have the power to change their beloved adult's feeling state, that they can make mummy 'sad / mad / bad' etc. Thinking back to the concept of encouraging differentiation between you and your child's ego state, we do not want to hammer home the idea that a child is responsible for a parent's emotions, we want them simply to grasp the idea that their actions can have emotional impact on others. It can be extremely counterproductive for a child to constantly hear, 'You are making Mummy sad.' This will result in them internalising a message that the child needs to mask or adapt their own feeling states in order not to make the parent feel bad.

Aged 5–8

At this age children have moved to a basic understanding of empathy; this does not mean they fully grasp it, but they do understand that other people's feelings can be hurt by the things we do or say. This is also the age where children start school and begin to realise that social interactions are not only between two people but also in a group. They understand that alliances can be formed and that things like social inclusion and exclusion exist. Generally, children at this age focus their friendships on shared experiences. We will see an increase in whole class engagement, whereas in the later primary school years we will start to see friendships breaking off into shared interests and individual personality choices.

This is likely the beginning of conversations where your child will come to you and tell you about social dilemmas or anxieties they are having. These are key learning moments to start sharing ideas about empathy in others – we do this at this stage very gently.

You have had a difficult time with that friend lately, what do you think they are feeling about what happened today?

A great way to explain the perspective of others to children is to introduce the idea of 'just me' thinking and 'thinking about others'. Here we are trying to encourage a developmental shift from looking only at our own lived experiences and to begin to consider the needs of others. This may not sound important when looking at individual trauma, but teaching empathy helps our children to start to understand their own emotional needs. They start to understand that emotions are connected to events, that human interaction can be both a balm and a cause of trauma, and it also helps them to start articulating emotions.

Children often connect to the idea of cost and reward, so if we are teaching a new way of behaving, we need to explain the benefit to that child. Children at this age are aware that others do have thoughts about them, and like adults they want those thoughts to be positive, so we can promote the idea of empathetic thinking as being a key component of friendship-making and friendship-maintaining. This is not to say that we encourage children to maintain friendships where they are being bullied or traumatised, and we will specifically cover bullying in the next chapter. Ways we might phrase this could be:

> *When we act like a just-me person, we want things done our way, we want to go first, we want people to only listen to us. But when we think of others, we try to help everyone be heard, and make everyone feel comfortable. This makes people feel happy to be around us.*

Aged 10–14

Pre-teens are likely much more aware of the concept of other people's feelings, and they also likely have a more astute sense of what other people think of them. This is a good age to start introducing the concept of other people's lived experience. In other words, we only see a slice of what is going on for that person. We don't need to ask our child to play psychoanalyst to other children here, but we can encourage them to think about the whole person rather than the one action they showed today that annoyed them. Ways we might phrase this:

> *I hear that was what you felt at the time, but I am wondering what he was thinking when he did that?*
>
> *I agree with you, that wasn't fair, but I'm interested to hear what you felt she felt about that?*

We are not encouraging our child to excuse or condone maltreatment or poor behaviour towards them, we are asking

72

them to tell us why they think the other person might have behaved the way they did, or what they felt about it. We are trying to increase a skill, known in psychology as 'mindsight' – the ability to view another person's emotional state.

PARENT TIP FOR CONFLICT: THE DISARMING SMILE AND SETTING BOUNDARIES

I teach this technique to parents of children with challenging behaviour, but it's also amazing for children of any age, including teens. We want to get our children into the prefrontal cortex when dealing with conflict, rather than firing the emergency response system – the limbic system (see page 17). So, we smile.

Why? Because a smile is a sensory cue we learnt as a baby that symbolises safety. The limbic system can call off the dogs, there is no threat (i.e. anger) being displayed here. Please note we do NOT use this as a manipulation technique – we do not smile when we are angry. Anger is an important human emotion and we do not teach our children to disguise it by smiling.

However, we use this disarming smile when we are setting boundaries. Let me repeat, we do not use the disarming smile to disguise anger, we use it to set boundaries.

Smiling helps send a signal to our brain that we are safe, and in turn tells the other person they are safe with US. Research suggests it's almost impossible to not smile back at someone who smiles at you – we have been hardwired as babies to return positive facial expressions. When we smile at our child while reminding them of the boundaries, we are reminding them, 'You are safe here, but I set boundaries. Boundaries keep us all safe, and my job as a parent is to protect you.'

Smile, then set the boundary. You might still be met with a large amount of resistance to the boundary, but then use the following:

I get you don't like it, you don't have to. This is the rule.

Why do we say, 'You don't have to like it'? Because we are enforcing the idea that boundaries are not there to win affection, they are there for safety. Also, we are fully competent adults who appreciate that anger, disappointment and frustration are a normal human emotion and we are not swayed by them. We are capable of holding all of the emotions our child's developing brain has to offer. I like to tell my children:

If you are angry, that's OK. All of you is welcome here.

No parent jumps into the role of parenting with ease and excellence, everyone has to go through a period of trying to find their way among a sea of confusing messages and internal triggers. Staying calm and consistent in the face of triggers is like training a muscle – the more often we do it, the stronger it becomes. It also becomes intrinsic and we begin to respond through muscle memory in a calm, controlled way. We develop our stock phrases to save us when we are floundering, and a few to help us when we are drowning. Children will thank you for your clear, consistent boundaries: stick with it.

Boundaries are key in any relationship, but none more so than a parent–child relationship. Teens and children want you to be in control. They may not act like they do, but they feel safer knowing someone is steering the ship. When they think the adult is unpredictable or not fully in control, they start trying

74

to take control themselves, out of anxiety not out of aggression. Our children want to feel like they are protected, that someone is there when they need help. We do this by nurturing their independence but setting safety barriers.

AN ATTACHMENT 'CHECK-IN' IS YOUR GREATEST PARENTING TOOL!

An attachment check-in, as I am referring to it here, is one the best tools you will ever have in your parenting arsenal. We know by now the importance of attachment and how it is the fundamental basis for the way your child views themselves and the world (see chapter 3). Attachment is a lifelong process, it is not something that is a one-and-done approach – you do not simply parent with intention from age 0 to age 2 and think, 'My work on attachment is done here.' You need to carry on re-enforcing the attachment base in order to help the child have the resilience with which to tackle the problems they face in the world.

A child will always look for a safe place from which to explore and, once they identify this, they will feel able to take on greater challenges, experience failure and also push limits, because they are safe in the place they call home. This is absolutely key as our children grow, and we need to help them manage the bumps in the road life throws at them. We need to give them the core belief of 'I am safe, I am loved' in order for them to feel they can bounce back from whatever life throws at them. The below exercise is a great tip I often give to parents to feel empowered to boost or support strong attachments. You do not have to give huge amounts of time or focus for this, you just need 20 minutes.

The Magic 20 Minutes

How many of us have been in the middle of something and done an internal eye roll at the question, 'Can you play with me?' or, even better, 'Mum, I'm bored.' The most common thing from parents I hear is, 'I really love doing stuff with my child, I like the crafts, and the baking . . . but god I hate imaginative play.' I'm going to tell you a secret – that's OK, every parent gets tired of being princess Elsa – but I am going to tell you another one: you don't have to do it all day for it to count! It's just 20 minutes . . .

When your child comes up to you asking to play, or tells you they want yet another snack, or they are bored, what they are actually saying is, 'I need a little bit of connection.' This is your golden chance for quality attachment building. Turn to them, put down what you are doing and give them 20 minutes of your attention to play / make / talk about whatever it is they want to do. That's it: 20 minutes. I guarantee you that after those 20 minutes, the child will feel full and connected enough to play independently for the rest of the hour.

Think of a toddler in a playgroup – they are zooming around, seemingly ignoring the mother but occasionally they will come back to touch Mum, ask for a snack or sit on her lap. What they are exhibiting is the prime example of secure attachment: they are exploring from a 'safe base'. They are checking in with Mum and then running off again to have their adventure. This is what your older child needs when they come and ask you to play – they want to connect with their safe base before they return to their own wonderful little worlds. Parenting can feel like we are on a never-ending merry-go-round of performing, always having to 'show up'. Ultimately we are not perfect and that's what makes us all human and real. Bite-sized bonding can be pure gold for parents and children. Remember: you aren't striving for perfection all day, every day – that would be impossible, unrealistic and exhausting. You can show up in many different ways for your children, and 20-minute imaginative play sessions are a great way to escape from the real world and have some fun, knowing that you don't have to be Elsa again until tomorrow!

THE KEY MESSAGE OF TEACHING RESILIENCE

Teaching resilience is about helping a child acknowledge what they can control and what they cannot. There are many forces in this world that are outside of their (and our) locus of control. However, this does not mean we have to feel powerless and fearful. Instead, we learn to recognise what forces are outside of our control, such as other people's emotions, and wider life experiences, and we focus on what we can control, such as *our own* responses, our boundaries.

When we teach children that boundaries are important to respect, we model to them that boundaries are something they should EXPECT. People should not be ignoring their boundaries, and they should adhere to the boundaries of others. When we acknowledge this, we feel safe and more relaxed – this ultimately puts us in a more positive mindset and a more grounded space from which to deal with life's problems. The reality is we cannot control other people, and we will come across a lot of things in life that we don't like; we only have control over how we respond to them.

When we promote the idea that generally the world and the people in it are doing their best to be good people, we allow our child to focus on the positives while acknowledging that sometimes the negative will happen and that is not in their control. Yes, there are bullies in this world, but a lot of the time those bullies have been bullied – teaching this helps the child acknowledge this is not about them or their 'badness', it's about things outside of their control. What they can control is how they respond. They can choose to not allow that person's negative experiences to become part of their self-talk, they can acknowledge that the bully has more than likely had some difficult experiences, and what they are saying is not coming from a factual place but from a reactive one. Most likely a survival one.

We do not teach our children to ignore their own thoughts and feelings, but we encourage them to consider others also. Likewise, we do not teach them that the way to manipulate others is through negative emotion – their word is enough, they do not have to fight you as the parent in order to be heard. You will listen to them and you will respect them; they do not have to become oppositional to you in order to feel psychologically safe – you are an oak in their storm, you are not going anywhere and you are not concerned by their emotional tempest; your love never wavers. All of them is welcome here, you are not frightened nor recoiling from their big emotions; with you they are safe. This helps them to feel a safer base from which to tackle the world and the things that WILL happen to them, and are outside of their control.

Make resilience a part of your daily discussion. Since my children have been verbal, every night before bed I ask them what their favourite thing was today and their not-favourite thing. They ask me too. I do this in order to teach the idea that your not-favourite thing has as much space in this house as your favourite thing, all of you are welcome here. The good comes with the bad sometimes in life, and we don't need to fear that or back away from it. We can embrace a day that has been full of challenges and triumphs, light and shade – we do not need to divide emotions and experiences into ones we talk about and ones we don't. Give it a go and see how your children respond.

Another favourite saying of mine is that 'nothing is wasted in nature'. My daughter and I settled on this phrase after we watched a conservationist talk to us about the animal food chain; my daughter felt extremely distressed about those at the bottom of the chain and I will never forget the look on her face when the conservationist smiled and explained to her that every single part of the food chain goes into promoting life on earth; even the apex predator, when they die, feeds the soil that feeds the plants.

He calmly summarised in a single sentence the entire concept of the cyclical nature of life and death: Nothing is wasted in nature. I love this sentence as it reminds her (and me) that everything, the dark and the light, has its purpose and it all feeds into a wonderful tapestry. Life is full of diverse experiences, but all is a cycle, all is a journey, all is part of the anthology of you.

A NOTE ON HOW TO USE THIS BOOK IF YOUR CHILD IS NEURODIVERSE

The term neurodiverse encompasses a number of diagnoses and labels that can be applied to a number of different developmental, communication and mental disorders. For the sake of this book we will be including the labels of autism spectrum condition

(ASC), ADHD, dyslexia, dyspraxia and dysgraphia. As this book is focused upon children and trauma, the other diagnoses that are sometimes included within the neurodivergent umbrella – such as bipolar, schizophrenia and schizoaffective disorder – are largely not diagnosed in the paediatric population. Child psychiatrists will refer to any symptoms that fall under these categories as 'emerging' or 'early onset' in patients under 18, so for that reason this section of the book will focus primarily on autism spectrum conditions and ADHD when using this label. There will be some reference to the childhood behavioural disorder known as oppositional defiant disorder (ODD), though this is not considered a neurodiverse condition by some.

Why am I including specific notes on neurodiverse children? Because as any parent of a neurodiverse child will tell you, there is no one-size-fits-all approach in anything. We know too that for many of these conditions there is a neurological component involving heightened stress responses and over-active fight / flight responses. Also because research shows that neurodiverse people are more likely to develop PTSD as a result of traumatic experiences, but most of all because being neurodiverse in a neurotypical world carries traumatic memories.

Let me tell you a story. I was recently diagnosed as being neurodiverse. I went through the initial shock and grief process that many adults who are diagnosed with neurodiversity are faced with. It made so much sense, and with that came huge relief, but it also felt a little heartbreaking. All these years I had managed this condition without help or understanding, and maybe if I had known this 20 years ago things could have been different. But now as a fully rounded and accepting ADHD woman, I have begun to recognise the sensory triggers that have caused me huge overwhelm in a variety of settings, but I also began to be aware of how well I have kept this hidden.

Recently I was in a training course with a number of other therapists, and we were sitting in a circle having a group supervision session. The delegate next to me was demonstrating something to the group and, in doing so, was repeatedly moving her hands in front of my face. I winced initially and hoped she would notice I was extremely uncomfortable with this 'invasion of space' as I saw it; she didn't. The hand waving became closer and more intense, and now all I could think was, 'I need this to stop, I don't like this.' Next came the irritation and the sense of wanting to get away. I could no longer engage in what this woman was saying; my brain was swamped with feelings of overwhelm and the chasing angry message of 'just stop doing this'.

I was then faced with the realisation that if I wanted this woman to stop gesturing near my face, I would have to say something. This was met with an internal moment of sheer panic – how on earth was I going to do that? What would everyone think? What would this woman think? How could I say this without coming across as impatient or intolerant? How could I casually explain this completely non-threatening gesture was in fact really distressing to me? Also, I was in a room of other professionals – what would people think of me that I could not 'contain' myself like they could?

So what did I do? What I always do in these situations: I said nothing. And that was when it hit me – being neurodiverse in a neurotypical world is traumatic. I said nothing because I had countless other times in my memory recall that I did say something and was met with confusion, ridicule or punishment. To describe the neurodiverse to a neurotypical person is, I am sad to say, rarely met with compassion. Neurodiverse adults know this so well that they likely have countless incidents in their own recollection of traumatic experiences of being made to feel weird, unreasonable, demanding or inappropriate just for being them. So I wanted to include these notes throughout the book with the loving acknowledgement to all neurodiverse adults and children that living with your beautiful neurodivergent brain in a neurotypical world comes with its own trauma.

Your child might have a diagnosis of ADHD or ASC, or something in between. In these circumstances where your child or a friend of your child has atypical behaviour, and some things may not come easily to them – such as reading social cues or deviating from a certain routine – it is wise to try to find a compromise where the child can feel safe and happy. It is also helpful in these cases to help those around the child be aware of the challenges their friend faces and how they can help. This models a wonderful lesson in empathy and developing compromise skills, and would be of great benefit to all involved.

With ASC children it could be the case that finding this compromise might require a little bit of adult involvement, but that doesn't mean to say that you can't encourage resilience. For children with ASC, the world is a very intense place and comes with a lot of unspoken rules and cues that don't always make sense. By helping them to navigate their own way in this strange and confusing universe, you are building resilient little spirits who embrace their challenges and find a path around them. We will look at some direct examples of how to manage these conversations with neurodiverse children.

Diagnoses of neurodiversity have increased greatly in the latter decade, and while many feel that this increase in diagnoses has brought with it some unhelpful over-medicalisation of certain children, many would also concur it has led to a positive step in greater research into these types of behaviours. A diagnosis of ADHD or ASC is now far more accessible, for example, and there is significantly greater understanding outside of the medical community about what these diagnoses mean. I am always heartened to see the rise in 'sunflower badges', which I see going about my day-to-day clinical work in London; this lovely initiative has been designed to help signify to the world around that this person has 'unseen' disabilities. No longer do ASC people have to go into lengthy and possibly painful explanations about why certain sensory issues trigger them; they can show their challenges discreetly.

Even more heart-warmingly, I am seeing a greater rise in literature and media celebrating neurodiversity. It is starting to be understood as not simply a 'condition' that brings with it problems and challenges, but a situation that can award the individual with incredible gifts – hyper-focus in the case of ADHD, for example, and wonderful creative problem-solving skills in the case of ASC. We do not need to assume that because someone has dyslexia, for example, that they can't produce creative writing – in fact we know that many of our greatest literary brains actually are dyslexic! Equally, just because someone has dyspraxia it doesn't mean that they cannot thrive in sports that don't require certain types of co-ordination. Neurodiversity is simply difference and variety, it is not necessarily a disability and it is not something that people need to feel stigma or shame over. For anyone who wishes to know, I am a proud ADHD 'sufferer' and I wouldn't change my diverse brain for the world.

However, we can assume that neurotypical children (in other words, children without conditions such as ADHD or ASC) might find some things a little bit easier than their atypical friends: it is likely they can interpret social cues more accurately, and that they don't find deviation from structure as distressing, but this doesn't mean that they don't also find the world a confusing and tumultuous place.

Trauma that comes from being neurodiverse

Being neurodiverse means living in a world of potential sensory triggers: the sound of someone eating, the sensation of someone's bag touching you, the lights in a classroom. All of these are potential sources of overwhelm. Neurodiverse people learn very early in life that society rarely accommodates their sensory concerns and will minimise or invalidate their distress. So the neurodiverse person attempts to mask their distress, and in doing so their nervous systems suffer a short circuit.

Why? Because the law of thermodynamics that governs the energy exchange of all atoms on earth says: energy never goes away or dies, it is converted to something else. This is important to understand when we think about trauma responses, as when the body does not successfully shake off or relieve itself of an adrenaline response it does not go away! It stays in the body, converted to a different type of energy.

Humans are considered to all have a 'window of tolerance' – this is where our body and mind are in a calm state and we can go about our day. If a threat presents itself we may go in to hyperarousal, where our nervous system sends us signals to 'react'. Hopefully we can then see off this threat via our fight / flight response and we can go back to our window of tolerance. If the threat appears overwhelming the body may go into hypoarousal, where it shuts down entirely and appears to play dead.

Sometimes we fear acting on our natural impulses to fight / flight as we worry about appearing scared or angry, so we attempt to ignore our nervous system signals. This energy is then converted to anxiety or stress as the body cannot complete the cycle of the nervous system response; we are then stuck in a space of adrenaline converting to cortisol and having nothing to do about it.

Both ADHD and ASC brains have been shown in a huge amount of research to present with higher levels of cortisol than neurotypical people and an atypical functioning of nervous system stress response. Neurodiverse brains likely enter a state of hyperarousal more quickly, and likely find it more difficult to return to a window of tolerance. Neurodivergent people are suggested by one study to be four times more likely than neurotypical people to develop PTSD following a trauma (Rumball et al.: 2020).

How to talk to your neurodiverse child about being neurodiverse

When dealing with neurodiversity and trauma, first and foremost you need to arm your children with the knowledge about what it means to be neurodiverse. (ADHD and ASC both require a formal diagnosis via a structured form of interviews and test, conducted by a paediatric professional such as a child psychiatrist, clinical psychologist or paediatrician.)

- Explain to them what is special and wonderful about their brain. Children with neurodiversity will face a lifetime of being told how their 'condition' is a disability and a disadvantage, so use this opportunity to reframe that narrative as one of positivity. Neurodiversity is a wonderful gift to many. For example, while my ADHD means that I struggle to locate car keys and I cannot reverse park or remember the dates of appointments, it gives me what my daughters and I refer to as 'Mummy's magic focus'. This helps to produce greater outputs of work or tasks than my non-ADHD husband and has been a big factor in my academic and professional successes.

- Offer an 'evolutionary' explanation of neurodiversity: evolutionary psychologists have suggested that neurodiversity has been positively selected by evolution for its traits that enable wonderful leaders. In a time of hunter-gatherers, tribes needed people who could search for new camps, pre-empt danger faster than others, develop new ways of doing things via intense, focused activity. These people were crucial to the survival of the tribe! People with neurodiversity who do not conform to the average population standards made for great leaders and inspiring minds. Neurodiverse people can harness their powers to be incredible shepherds of change and thought leadership – they have exceptional talents!

- Find as many examples as you can of inspiring artists, leaders, athletes and creatives who have neurodiverse traits as an example to show your child that this is a heightened ability not a disability. Use media, books and TV programmes that celebrate diversity as much as possible.

CHAPTER 5:
EXTRACT–
EXPRESS–
REFLECT

Extract–Express–Reflect is a technique I have developed based on a psychological tool known as 'debriefing'. If you take nothing else away from the book, I hope you will remember this simple technique and keep it in your back pocket for whenever you are facing difficulty alongside your child.

Debriefing is a structure of questions designed to be asked immediately after a traumatic event, with the goal of preventing the development of PTSD and other negative impacts. Debriefing came about in the 1990s and is not without its critics, most of whom say that PTSD cannot be prevented by a simple questioning technique. I would agree with them in the sense that we know some individuals – particularly those from a poor attachment base – are more likely than others to develop PTSD. But nonetheless I do feel that this particular technique is extremely useful when assisting children in processing little t traumas, and we would not necessarily use it following a big T trauma – PTSD prevention is not our aim here. What we are going for is traumatic impact reduction.

When debriefing first responder teams, psychologists generally follow a seven-step process where they assess the incident, identify safety issues / learnings, allow emotional expression, share others' emotional reactions, reflect on the impact, re-enter the workplace / community. My technique is a much more distilled version of this, where in the first section we extract all the information, then following this we ask the child to express the thoughts and feelings they have about that information and then we help the child to reflect on their own experiences with the event, and how they can instil a sense of empowerment in themselves after this has happened to them.

EXTRACT

At this stage, we are looking to get all the who / what / where information with as much detail as possible. We do this for a very specific reason: research tells us that emotional reactions are stored in a very specific way by the limbic centre (the emotional centre) of the brain, and memories that are traumatic or include the emotions of fear, disgust or distress can sometimes be overwhelmed by the limbic centre and not make their way into the prefrontal cortex (the reasoning and logical section of the brain). Crucially, when memories stay locked in the limbic centre, they are often poorly verbalised because they haven't been able to be processed by the verbal reasoning section of the brain: the prefrontal cortex.

So when we extract, we are trying to ensure that the prefrontal cortex fires up and engages all the sensory information it gathered, and files it away properly; we don't want to miss this part and allow the memory to go straight to the limbic system, as we know it might then get stuck in processing limbo.

EXPRESS

Next, we want to express all the emotion. Again, here we are making sure the emotion centre is speaking to the reasoning centre. We don't want anything left out; we want to hear all the emotions that accompanied this memory so nothing gets stuck in processing or hidden away.

It is not always easy for children to name emotions, so a good place to start is, 'How do you feel in your body?' By naming body sensations, you can encourage children to start thinking about what is going inside them. Younger children might need a little help with this, so you can ask questions such as, 'How does your heart feel – is it very fast?', or, 'How does your chest (point to it) feel?'

From here, help the child to name the emotion that connects to that body sensation – do not make the mistake of thinking that all anxiety is fear or that all tears are sadness. Tears can signify anger, and rage can signify shame. Ask questions and, if you are unsure, a good question to use is, 'Is it more like X or Y?' So take two emotions that you think the child might be holding, such as fear and anger, and ask, 'Which one do you feel more, anger or fear?' Try to dig deep into the emotion that is being potentially repressed as well as the one that is being expressed.

For example, many children will say they feel angry or they hate something when they feel embarrassed. Equally, many children will show sullenness or apathy when they feel sadness.

REFLECT

Lastly, we want to reflect. Now, unlike the standard debriefing technique you would do with adults, here I focus very specifically on two things: what the child did, and what control they have in the situation. A lack of control or feeling helpless is a common negative belief following a little t or big T trauma.

A key part of this technique is to encourage the child to focus not only on what they did which was positive, but also on the positive actions of others, where relevant. When we encourage our child to see the 'helpers' in the world we are actively challenging any negative thoughts setting in, such as 'people are bad', 'the world is a dangerous place', 'I can't trust people'. This helps to keep them positive and it also helps them to maintain a positive belief in others, which we know helps to promote self-esteem.

We don't know why some people get negative beliefs of self after a traumatic event and some don't, but what we do know is that PTSD research shows that the feeling of being a 'bystander' is one of the key components to developing this. Let me explain. Research with combat veterans showed that those who were deployed on missions that involved harm to civilians or non-combatants were more likely to develop PTSD than those in active warfare. Research also tells us that a soldier under 25 is seven times more likely to develop PTSD than an older veteran.

So what can we take away from this? Younger brains struggle more to process trauma and, crucially, 'I could have done more

/ why didn't I do . . .' are key internal messages for developing trauma impact. So in our reflect section of this technique, our primary goal is to help the child notice and articulate all the great things THEY did, as we know in the case of any trauma (big T or little t) a key component of stopping negative internal messages is promoting the idea of self-agency and self-esteem.

TIMING

One of the key theories of debriefing following a traumatic interaction or experience is to do it as soon as possible after the event. In fact trauma debriefing is done 48–72 hours after the event; later than this and it is referred to as 'trauma counselling', as the body and the brain have already begun to form a narrative and to process the information they have about the event. We would like to avoid the body doing this, as we want to ensure that the body processes two things: the facts, and a positive message. Without the assistance of debriefing, the body may only store fragmented memory, and potentially more negative messages about their own role in the memory, than if they have the assistance of a debriefer. The debriefer's role is to add perspective and context to the memory so the survivor can feel they have an accurate narrative of what happened and what they did.

When your child has had something happen to them that has produced an emotional reaction in them such as shame, fear or shock, it is absolutely crucial that you find the first feasible time available to you to debrief this with them. It does not necessarily have to be straight away, but it has be as close to the event as possible (ideally the same day, but as soon as possible is our goal). If we allow the memory to be stored as a fragmented memory the child may still experience the physical reminders of the memory (the body triggers) but they may not have stored the memory accurately and, more importantly, they may embed a negative message around blame or failure in relation to themselves. We want to prevent this.

SETTING YOUR SPACE

Attention to space and setting makes the difference in the quality of our interactions with another – if you want someone to feel they can 'talk', consider the environment in which you are asking them to 'talk' in. Never attempt to initiate a difficult discussion with someone in a space that feels punitive, where they cannot leave easily, where they feel overheard, or where they feel they haven't given consent to be there. Paying attention to the surroundings and your body position in relation to another can take a conversation from closed off and defensive to open and inviting.

When someone is in shock, the first thing you do is take them to a place of safety; this is likely to be somewhere away from visual reminders of the trauma, and if possible audible reminders. So, using the example of a child who has slipped into a swimming pool and was pulled out quickly: pick the child up, to provide an immediate sense of physical safety (being held) and take the child fully away from the poolside to help calm their feelings of shock and fear.

In the case of a child who has witnessed an accident or an adult argument that has scared them, remove them entirely from the scene and do not begin to debrief with them until they are in a place where they can no longer see reminders of the event. If a child is telling you about a shameful or humiliating experience that happened at school, do not debrief with them on the school run or in the playground. Wait until the child feels entirely comfortable and safe.

So how do we set a space where a child feels safe? An ideal location to debrief in is the room of their choosing where they feel their happiest. For many children this will be their bedroom, for others it might be another room. But the key message here is a place that a) is known, b) contains happy memories, c) is predictably safe. When I say predictably safe, I am focusing here on a place a child can reasonably assume people will not come in to disturb the talk, and they do not feel confined or restrained in any way.

You may not be in the position of being close to your home or the child's bedroom when you debrief, so how do we create a 'safe space' on the run? You as the parent will have to use your own physicality to create an environment: hold the child, look at their face, speak in clear and soothing words to remind them, 'I am here.' I often repeat to my own children, 'Mummy is here, Mummy has got you,' when doing this exercise just to instil an idea of safety and control. The key message is to remind them that 'this place is safe, and you are safe here'. We cannot reasonably expect someone to share with us in a place that feels unprotected.

So find a location AWAY from the trigger as much as possible; ideally the space should be as private as possible and without noise or distractions. Where possible, get grounded: sit down somewhere comfortable and create a feeling of sanctuary and safety. Another nice tip is to offer warmth by way of a blanket or coat, even if the child doesn't say they feel cold. Offer as many ways as possible to create protection and warm surroundings. You can also offer a drink to help with any dry mouth and to prevent hyperventilating breathing.

SET THE TONE WITH YOUR BODY AND VOICE

We have already discussed the importance of using your body to provide safety and warmth, particularly following a period of shock. But be conscious of your body language; do not appear distracted or in a hurry. Focus on trying to show:

1. Time (*there is time . . . there is space . . .*)
2. Tone (*I am interested in what you to have to say but I am not shocked*)
3. Temper (*I have no agenda here, I am calm, big feelings do not scare me*)

When trying to teach Time, Tone, Temper to people I ask them to hold in mind the following words: 'I am here to help you.' By repeating these words to ourselves we automatically become more patient, less agitated and more conscious to appear non-judgemental. Even if we are struggling with our responses to what the child is telling us, by repeating this in our head we can keep the focus on the child and not on our own feelings. It is crucial that we approach our child from a place of interest (we need to be interested in order to 'extract' the information), safety (we need to be welcoming and accepting of all the emotions that may come) and with no agenda (we need to help the child find in THEMSELVES the message of 'I am in control'; we do not force our own message on to them).

Showing you have time to listen and to help means not interrupting, allowing for spaces of silence, and not pre-empting answers. Many parents find this part of the technique straightforward, as many aspects of parenting require patience and this is no different. However, one of the more challenging parts of this technique is to show interest. Why? Because you have to ask exploratory questions in a curious manner, in the form of a researcher, rather than in the form of 'getting to the story'.

What does this look like? Many parents will jump straight to, 'Tell me what happened,' and finish there, but what we want is not to simply hear 'what happened', but all the details of the memory. We want to know where the child was standing, who was around them, what their faces looked like, what they were feeling, who said what. This is wonderful contextual information that helps the brain to kick into 'processing mode'. Most importantly, we want to keep asking what happened next.

Let's take for example a child who saw a car accident. We want to say something like, 'Ah, OK, so you were waiting at the bus stop and then you saw the red car come round the corner and hit the blue car . . . then what happened?' (Mirror back the response): 'OK, so afterwards you heard all the people screaming and then you saw the lady running . . . what did she do?' (Mirror back the response): 'So the lady said to the man to call an ambulance and then someone called 999. What were you thinking?' (Mirror back the response): 'Ah OK, so you were worried about the man in the car and you were scared of the shouting . . . then what happened?'

In the above example we want to show that we are constantly

checking in for the details of facts and feelings and also moving the narrative on. We don't want the narrative to get stuck on one place, we want to process the whole story.

Managing temper is important as the story progresses as we need to be careful to not appear to have a 'line of questioning' – in other words, we are not seeking an outcome. Children often worry that adults are seeking to tell them off, and they may be fearful of sharing something they think paints them in a bad light. So we need to appear non-judgemental at all times. Keep repeating the words, 'I am here to help you' in your head.

HOW TO DO EXTRACT–EXPRESS–REFLECT WITH NEURODIVERSE CHILDREN

While the principles of the technique will work with all children, with some children certain stages may take longer and require more processing time. Following the same principles as given earlier, get the child to express exactly what they saw and what happened, how they felt, and what this means to them now. A few points with neurodiverse children:

- The extract stage is likely to take longer with ADHD children as their narrative structure can be very jumbled and disjointed, particularly when in a state of distress. Help them along the way by creating a structure of events – write it down in order and get them to look at it in order to organise their thoughts: this happened, then this happened.
- With ASC children they will likely have a great ability to retain factual information; however, if they are

experiencing emotional shutdown as a result of the trauma, allow this to pass BEFORE you go into the extract stage.

- For the express stage ASC children will likely need a lot of help around what emotional vocabulary to use to express what they feel. Likewise, ADHD children may need help structuring their thoughts into a sequence BEFORE they get to the express stage, otherwise they may feel overwhelmed and be unable to name their emotions.

- For the reflect stage, both sets of children are able to offer a reflection on what this experience might mean for them, but give them space to formulate their thoughts in order to do so. They may need help to reframe their experience as a positive one – remembering that their nervous system takes longer to calm down and therefore they may still be in a state of emergency. They will need assistance to calmly and consciously decide on a positive narrative of growth.

- If you are struggling to find a positive narrative of growth, always look for the helpers! Focus on the who, what, when, where, why of things that helped or people who helped. You can draw out actions they took or things they said if they were alone in the event.

Extract–Express–Reflect example

When my eldest daughter was two, we lived in Hong Kong. Hong Kong is known for having horrendous typhoons, and during one such typhoon – the worst in 60 years – the entire ground floor of our house got flooded. My daughter had very little understanding of what was going on but she could hear the hurricane wailing outside, and she could see the adults in the house hurriedly trying to carry furniture upstairs to avoid the flood water. She could likely also sense the panic in the house.

Years later when we were walking through a park in London, she saw a tree had fallen down. Rather than playing on it, she panickily told me the entire story of that typhoon – how she had looked out of the window and seen her daddy wading through waist-deep storm water trying to save her trampoline that had blown into the tree, also the sound the tree branches made as the wind whipped them at the glass. She also told me that the next day, everywhere was a 'tree graveyard' – 500 trees were blown down. The sight of that tree in a park, in an entirely different country, three years later, brought back that memory to her. The funny thing was, I didn't even know she remembered that day as she couldn't even speak in complete sentences at the time.

It is important to remember that while children may not be able to articulate in narrative form what they have seen or done, their body 'remembers'. Therefore, it is important if we think that our child might be reacting strongly to a seemingly innocuous stimuli or memory, we consider the aspects of the memory and how they might relate to something in the past.

To give another example, one day when my daughters and I were walking our dogs, our dog Bob got stuck down a storm drain (he's a Labrador and he thought he saw a leftover McDonald's down there – what can I say?). We swiftly realised once he had fallen in that it was decidedly difficult to get him out again. At the time we were in a very remote jungle part of Hong Kong. I tried to throw logs down to help him get out, I tried to lower myself into the drain to get him out, but realised this would be too dangerous and, for a moment, I was really terrified. So was he and he began crying in a pitiful 'help me' way. The truth is, I didn't know what to do, and to make matters worse, we had no phone reception. Issy became aware of my panic and started to get very distressed.

A hiker came past and offered to help us. In the end she and I built a makeshift log ramp for Bob to run up and get himself out. Thanking this kind passer-by with a big hug, I turned immediately to Issy, knowing this would be an important memory, and possibly one that might be traumatic. I said to her, 'Tell me what just happened, Issy.' I encouraged her to tell me absolutely everything – who was where and what we did. After she retold me what she had just seen, I quickly turned the conversation focus to 'the lady that helped' and also 'how Issy had been helpful and brave'. The memory I wanted to embed in Issy's brain was one that was tinged with the positive memory of these aspects.

One of the most important things we can do when our children have dealt with something that was difficult or potentially traumatic is to enforce any positive learnings we can find – particularly those that emphasise the kindness of others or good judgement used by the child. To go back to Issy and the 'Bob in the drain' memory, she frequently recalled it every time we went past that spot, but I noticed she always followed the memory up with, 'That's where I kept watch on Bob, while you and the kind lady got some logs isn't it Mum?' Issy has now interpreted that memory as challenging but not traumatic, and this is key, because she has formed a narrative about the memory that gives her positive cognitions about the world: people are helpful, I am strong, I was in control, I am good in a crisis. I strongly encourage all parents to do the same when faced with difficult situations.

- Extract (all the information about who, what, where, why)
- Explain (get emotional detail, how did you feel, what did you think)
- Reflect (look here for positive learning, particularly focusing on helpful 'others' and the child's own positive choices)

LITTLE T TRAUMAS WITH BIG FEELINGS

Accepting the difficult realities of life is hard. We are simply not programmed to want anything other than the best possible outcome for ourselves, so others often frustrate, anger or irritate us when this doesn't happen – in some cases this might promote feelings of betrayal, loss or rejection. Children don't deal with these feelings any better than adults, and it's helpful for parents to remember that. Everybody can probably recall a time in the playground when someone did or said something that caused them embarrassment, hurt or anger, and the reason we hold on to those memories all those years later is that those feelings were very big and very real at the time. So when your child comes home and says that somebody caused them distress today, try to avoid minimising it with a 'don't worry' or, 'I'm sure they didn't mean it'. Of course children, like adults, can misinterpret others' actions but maybe the other child really did try to cause intentional hurt, and minimising that isn't going to help your child. What can help your child is reminding them straight away that you love them, and this is a space where they can share. These moments are prime opportunities to do an attachment 'check-in': I love you, you are safe.

Now the attachment re-enforcement has helped to lessen the sting of recalling the experience and reminded the child that they are in a safe, nurturing place to share all their difficult feelings, you can begin to ask a few questions to get the details of the incident. Once this conversation begins, it may well turn out that there is a different interpretation than the negative one your child feels, and now is a good time to gently offer another possible explanation without forcing. You could, for example, say, 'Maybe it was like this because he / she felt this today?' This can be a great teaching moment to encourage your child to consider the emotions of others. Here we are encouraging empathy, and modelling how empathy can form the basis of healthy, boundaried attachments with others.

After this teaching moment (if applicable), now is the time to ask your child to consider their own 'resources'. How might they have successfully dealt with something like this in the past? Or help them devise a creative way they might deal with this in future. This could be through role playing or modelling behaviour for future encounters, or it could be simply discussing different possibilities. Above all, model a hopeful attitude that next time things will have a positive outcome, and that your child will feel differently than they do today. Encourage the thought that change can always happen and it's not something to be scared of, so maybe this interaction will change certain things, but it might change them for the better. Particularly if this interaction might have given the child the opportunity to consider their own boundaries and how they can protect them kindly and confidently in the future.

Resilient people are people who approach life with a hopeful, positive attitude and who have a sense of their own agency (their own ability to create change) in their life. They are also people who empathically consider others and the situations that surround them that might promote certain responses. They are people who remind themselves regularly of the possibility that maybe 'it's not about me, the person had something else going on' and also, 'I am important and worthy of respect, I will show kindness and respect to others and I expect them to do the same for me.' Resilient people are also those who realise that sometimes this simply isn't going to happen, and the best course of action is to leave the situation and look for a more positive one elsewhere. Try to model this behaviour in your own life and set an example for your child to follow suit.

EXTRACT–EXPRESS–REFLECT IN PRACTICE

Extract–Express–Reflect is a great technique that can be done quickly and immediately following an event that you suspect your child found traumatic or distressing. It does not have to be done in a particular setting or by a professional, it is simply a three-step process that you can follow. In the next chapters I will explore a range of little t traumas to demonstrate how this technique can be applied in a range of circumstances. Unfortunately, I cannot cover all possible little t traumas in this book, but it should be a good jumping-off point for you to start building your toolkit for raising a resilient child.

- **Extract** the information in order for the memory to be filed by the brain accurately. This is absolutely key as we know that traumatic memories are often not stamped correctly with sequential data. When we ensure that we get the who, what, why, when out of the memory, we are forcing the brain to connect all the factual data to that memory, alongside the emotion, and trying to bypass the need for the brain to file the memory without correct factual data. Factual data can be key to proving or disproving theories around control or agency – for example, remembering the kind passer-by can help challenge any ideas setting in along the lines of 'nobody helped me.'

- **Express** the feeling, allow space for ALL the emotions! Let the anger, fear, shame or distress come out and get the child to verbalise it. This is key to not allowing the body to store the physical by-products of these emotions such as raised adrenaline. When we connect the emotion to the body sensation, we remove the brain's desire to inaccurately form a trigger between the memory and the body sensation. For example, when we encourage the child to say, 'When I saw that car crash, my throat tightened, my mouth was dry, and I felt shocked and scared,' we prevent the child connecting the later feeling, 'I heard a bang and my throat is tightening . . . maybe the car accident is happening again, I need to rush to survival mode, my adrenaline is racing . . . I'm terrified.'

- **Reflect** on the alternative views and outcomes. This is so key for looking at all the possibilities as it helps the child to consider what actually happened and what might have happened. It's important to allow this 'what might have happened' conversation as we may find what is stuck in this part of the reaction is the underlying fear. For example: 'That dog barked at me . . . but what I was really scared of was it was going to bite me . . . or maybe even what I was really, really, scared of was it was going to kill me.' We need to get to these more irrational beliefs in order to challenge them and rationalise them. When we don't do this, we allow the brain to form catastrophising connections between harmless triggers such as a dog, and an extreme fear connected to an irrational thought of a dog attack.

Reframe the memory into one of empowerment (look for the helpers in the story, look for the child's own sense of bravery or agency). This is one of the most important parts of this technique, to look for anything that promotes your child's self-esteem or self-agency in the memory, even if the connection is tiny, 'It was amazing that you knew to come and ask for help,' or, 'It was such a good decision to run away.' Trauma causes shame as a result of helplessness, and the antidote to shame is the message: you were in control, you made good choices.

Within every traumatic story there is a message of hope if you look hard enough. Even if the trauma has only been used as a source of learning or later self-protection. A trauma doesn't define you, it is a chapter in a book in the library of stories that you are.

CHAPTER 6: SEPARATION ANXIETY

One of the most famous child psychologists of all time, Donald Winnicott, whose research and writings led the way for later attachment theory (see chapter 3), did NOT berate mothers. He did not shame them, he did not set out to tell them all the 50 ways they damaged their child; he wanted to tell them that intent was everything, and that a perfect output was impossible. Now let me break it down what this meant in his terms: in the first part of a baby's life, the mother should make every ATTEMPT to respond to her child's cries and meet their need until gradually allowing minor, tolerable frustrations to be experienced, in order for the child to become independent. This is another key message I think gets lost in attachment parenting literature – Winnicott did not say you have to give 100 per cent of your life 100 per cent of the time to your child, he said it is a complex balancing act of meeting needs and gradually encouraging the child to meet them themselves. He introduced the idea of a 'good enough' mother, not the perfect mother, not the could-do-better mother: the good ENOUGH mother. I need to say it again to let it sink in.

As we saw in chapter 3, attachment theory was developed by John Bowlby, alongside Mary Ainsworth. In the 1970s, she devised an experiment to show what attachment looks like in real terms. Known as 'The Strange Situation', it involved a child entering a room with their mother, the mother leaving, and a stranger coming in; the stranger leaves and the mother returns, and all of this is observed by psychologists who attempt to map out the responses of the children into 'attachment patterns'. The four attachment patterns, or styles, to emerge (secure, anxious / ambivalent, avoidant, disorganised) are outlined on pages 54–8 and were held by Bowlby and Ainsworth to form a blueprint of how a child will relate to the world around them.

Why is this important in the definition of separation anxiety? Because separation anxiety is demonstrated during this exact experiment: the part where the parent leaves. But in order to understand separation anxiety we must hold in mind these two ideas: when a baby develops an idea of permanence, in other words an object exists, they hold in their mind that the object can be removed from them. Secondly, a securely attached child explores their surroundings safe in the knowledge that the mother *even if they cannot be seen by the child, or are not in proximity to the child* is still there to be attentive to their needs.

SEPARATION AND SLEEP TRAINING

When I had my second child, I remarked to a friend: 'Check out how often I get asked: so how is she sleeping?' My friend didn't understand this as a question – she was raised in a very rural part of SE Asia where babies are generally carried and sleep and fed at will. Confused, she replied: 'Why would anyone ask that? She's a baby.' 'Because,' I laughed, 'if there is one thing Western society is obsessed with, it's baby sleep patterns.' Sadly, the next few people we saw that day asked me the exact question, as I predicted.

I could waste this entire book telling you what I did and which of the sleep training camps I fall into, and justifying my reasons for each, but in the end what does it matter? I did what I needed to do to manage my life with my baby. (For anyone who really cares, I was a co-sleeper and an 'extended breastfeeder' as I realised recently my choice would be called. I made these choices as they felt right to ME, and for what it's worth I know fabulous mothers who did the complete opposite.)

I want therefore to be clear when I say separation anxiety is not created through your choice on how to put your child to sleep or how to feed them, it is created through a child's emotional response to your absence. There are of course certain styles of parenting that will help to bolster your child's emotional attachment, such as ensuring there is physical touch and closeness, especially during the baby years, that there is attentive eye contact and responsive nurturing. But there is no science behind any feeding or sleeping choice that prevents or causes separation anxiety. Separation anxiety can happen to children with wonderful mothers; it is categorically not caused by a 'bad' choice you have made.

WHAT IS SEPARATION ANXIETY?

Separation anxiety is a NORMAL developmental stage that occurs between the ages of six months and three years. It occurs when your child cries when their caregiver leaves, or they feel distressed to be cared for by a different person. This is a brain development stage where they notice:

1. Mum / Dad is a permanent object and they exist even when I can't see them. They go and they come back.
2. Mum / Dad is an important part of my safety and my survival: I need Mum / Dad.
3. When I cry, adults do things; this is a good way to convey my distress or try to communicate my needs.

Separation anxiety is managed through practised separation, by leaving your child with another caregiver (preferably someone they already have a relationship with) for short periods of time. Stick to a schedule and return as communicated. Even with pre-verbal children, explain in short, easy to understand sentences, such as: 'I am going to do this now, but I will be back in one hour.'

Keep the surroundings familiar where possible; this will help to create a feeling of stability and known safety. Also: do not draw out the goodbye, and have a noticeable ritual that signifies goodbye, such as a goodbye song or a kiss / cuddle.

More than anything, be predictable: return as agreed, and try to develop a 'return ritual' that reminds your child you are back now and everything is 'normal' again. Everyone is safe. Do not discount your child's feelings by saying things like 'don't cry', try to stick to 'Mummy is going but Mummy will return.'

Make separations easy and relaxed – but predictable – and let your child grow into the idea that sometimes adults have to go somewhere, but they come back. Also that sometimes I can go to places without them, like school or a play date, and I come back too. Coming and going is OK, there's always a safe space to return to.

WHAT IS SEPARATION ANXIETY DISORDER?

Separation anxiety disorder is when separation anxiety is either developmentally unexpected (i.e. after six years old) or is intense enough to interfere with normal daily functioning. Separation anxiety disorder is characterised by a marked distress or extreme fear response when the primary caregiver leaves. It can also be characterised by thoughts or excessive worry about something bad happening to them or the caregiver during the separation period. These fears could be anything from imagining illness, death, kidnap or natural disasters. It can also manifest as fear to go to sleep or refusal to go to school.

Symptoms of anxiety disorder can include:

- physical clinging on to caregiver, such as holding a leg or blocking the exit
- stomach aches or headaches that occur prior to the separation
- excessive tantrumming or crying
- head banging or self-harming
- excessive nightmares about separation due to an extreme event or permanent event, such as natural disaster or death

Separation anxiety disorder does not occur after one episode or emotional outburst, it is recurrent, and it prevents normal daily functioning in order to be considered a disorder. There can be many causes for separation anxiety disorder and some can be:

- previous trauma, particularly one that causes threat of harm to caregiver
- change in environment such as home or school
- divorce or separation
- loss, such as a death in the family or family pet
- insecure attachment pattern

Practical tips for managing distress around separation

- Keep calm during separation moments. Remember the mantra 'children do what we do not what we say' – we have to be the calm in the chaos at all times, but never more so than when a child feels distress. Prepare yourself for the moment by taking some deep breaths, centre yourself and mentally remind yourself that 'everything is OK, I am safe'.
- Practise the routine. What is known instils familiarity. Familiarity helps instil safety. Practise the way you will leave, discuss the amount of time you will be apart and talk about what you will both do in between. Plan the return.
- Have a comforting and grounding ritual to do when you return. Think of it as something to look forward to that helps to reconnect.

PARENTING IN SEPARATION ANXIETY DISORDER

There is a connection between overly anxious parenting, or 'overprotective' parenting and anxiety disorders in children – in this instance a child is mirroring the parent's anxiety about being separated from them. They have picked up the message from the parent that stress is felt when we are apart and interpreted this as: 'It's dangerous to be away from my parent. I can see in their eyes that it is unsafe.'

If this is you, then firstly, it is not your fault, and this situation can be dealt with. It is highly likely that you have a very good reason to feel fearful or stressed at the thought of being separated from your child. Maybe you suffered from previous trauma and you feel terrified of something similar happening to your child, or maybe you suffer from other anxiety conditions that make it very hard to manage your biological responses to stressful thoughts. In these instances, you are trying to protect your child from the unseen dangers of the world that are very real in your head. You may feel plagued with thoughts of terrible things happening, or imagining the world as a very dangerous place. Your child senses that 'see danger' in many places and interprets the world as a similarly unsafe place.

Maybe you are naturally very self-critical and punish yourself for separating from your child by telling yourself you are a bad parent for working / taking time for yourself or simply existing. This may then cause you to micromanage your child or to feel overly critical towards teachers or other caregivers. The child then notices this critique of others, particularly those who have a caretaking role of them, and then interprets these people as unsafe.

If you feel that any of the above is reflective of you, or you recognise other origins of your child's separation anxiety disorder in your parenting, then get professional help for your own mental health. As they always say on airline safety briefings, attend to your own oxygen mask first: make sure you are secure before you attempt to soothe your child. Children are emotional sponges who copy what we do and not what we say. If you show your child a 'dangerous' world, don't be surprised when they feel fearful.

SEPARATION ANXIETY ABOUT PLACES (MOVING HOUSE / SCHOOL)

I wanted to put something in here about a child's feelings of anxiety around the loss of a place. This is a subject very close to my own heart as we as a family have moved countries four times. When we left Hong Kong, where both of my children were born, I was overwhelmed with anxiety and sadness about taking my girls away from the only home they had ever known, particularly my eldest as she was four at the time and could grasp the concept of leaving. I sat in this sadness and feeling of loss for a number of weeks after I realised we were going to be leaving, and I mourned for my own losses of friends, memories and also the early years of my child's life. More than anything I wondered what I was going to do about Issy – how could I help her manage these hard emotions?

A good friend who was a therapist recommended that I write her a story, so that's what I did. I wrote Issy a story about a little elephant who kept lots of things in a box in order to remember them, and he moved homes only to feel that unless he had a full memory box of 'things', he would forget his home. The mummy elephant reminded him that memories exist inside our hearts and not in our possessions and we could carry lots of memories throughout our life and all its changes.

I now use the book when working with children with separation anxiety to help them understand that we don't need to grip on to something in order to show it we love it or that it is special to us. I also use it to help children understand loss as a result of environmental change. Even if you didn't go so far as to move continents as my family did, environmental change happens to children all the time. Schools, houses, hobbies, houses of family members — all of these things are regular transitions in children's lives, and we don't always acknowledge that a change in environment can feel a loss to a child.

We can see this 'environment loss' in children who constantly compare their new place to the old one, and find negative associations with the new compared to the old. We can also see this in children who appear more withdrawn in the new environment or no longer find things they enjoy. It's common to see an emergence of nightmares in children who have moved house, and it's very common to see a change in personality for children who have moved schools.

It's so important to allow children to acknowledge that their 'old place' was one in which they felt safe, and in this 'new place' feelings are unknown and maybe a little bit frightening.

Tips for managing separation anxiety about places

- Plan ahead and do your research together. Take time to learn about, talk about and if possible visit this new place. So if you are moving to a new area, take your child to explore it with you. What shops are there? What new things can you do there? What are the things that you can continue doing there (such as places for their hobbies or enjoyed pursuits)?

- Plan new routines together, practise the new school run and think about things you can bring from the 'old place' and also things you might want to be totally new for the 'new place'.

- If you are moving countries or large geographical distances, try to connect with families in the area or clubs that might be interesting to your child – ahead of time. Help your child to feel part of a community before they arrive, so that some things will feel 'known' to them. Invest time in building some social connections for your child so that they feel they have someone they know.

- Allow space to mourn the things you will miss but also the things you are looking forward to. Try to find the gains as well as recognising the losses in this change. Don't focus purely on the positives or the negatives; help children to see that change contains both, and that is OK.

- Pick out some 'new things' – maybe that is a new school bag, or asking for their help to decorate their new room. Try to find a way to include your child in the change and give them some sense of control and agency within it.

EXTRACT–EXPRESS–REFLECT FOR SEPARATION ANXIETY

Extract

One of the most important parts of managing separation anxiety is to look at the context in which it occurs. So, for example, look at the time of day, the activity, who is involved, what has happened before the response, and what is the history of this response. This is very important when dealing with anxiety responses, as nine times out of ten the current 'activation' of their nervous system, in other words the trigger, comes from a previous experience. It is rare to see anxiety reacting to something that is happening 'now' – it is usually a reaction to a trauma that has passed.

For example, your child may become anxious before a weekday bedtime, but when prompted will start to talk about when they were separated from you previously. So, given we are managing an anxiety response in this example, one of your key things to extract is the answer to the question: 'When have you felt this before?' Encourage your child to share the exact details that cause them anxiety; remind them they don't need to 'explain' why, as they don't need to have a rational basis, but just focus on the question 'tell me the worst part', so you can drill down into what exactly is causing the trigger.

Good discovery questions might be:

- Can you tell me where in your body you feel the feeling (don't refer to it as anxiety at this stage)? Listen carefully to the answer: the underlying emotion may not be fear, it might be sadness or anger.

- That sounds like it might be (name an emotion), does that sound right?
- What's the worst part of the thought? (Don't refer to it as anxiety or fear unless they use that word.)
- So it sounds like when X happens you feel Y?
- When was the first time you ever felt this body feeling (go with the physical feeling not the emotion)?
- Was that the worst time? (Stick here with the body sensation NOT the emotion . . . it's the physical trigger response we want to identify the origin of.) Some children won't be able to remember but give them space to think and also offer suggestions of times you think they MIGHT have felt this previously.

Express

Once you think you have identified the trigger response, you can start to dig into the emotion around it. It is key to lead with the body feeling, as this is the biological cause of anxiety: for example, feeling tightness in the chest, sweaty palms, shaky legs are all examples of anxiety response, and times where these physical sensations have been experienced may relate to the current feeling. Whereas anger, sadness or fear are wide-ranging emotions and may be applied to a number of situations that have nothing to do with this anxiety. Sticking with body sensations helps keep the exploratory questions focused, and also helps your child to recognise where in their body they feel this.

Once this has been identified, start to talk about what it feels like to have that physical feeling, what are the thoughts that go with it? For example, 'So when you start getting hot inside and your throat starts to feel squeezed, you get worried what is going to happen next.' Remind the child at all times that their physical responses are normal and nothing to fear: 'I feel that too when I do XYZ.' 'That feeling in your heart is your body telling you it wants to run away, so it's making your heart beat very fast.'

If you have managed to identify the first example in the child's life of feeling this sensation, explore that narrative. Get them to tell you as a story what happened 'when I was five and you left to go to work and I . . .' Listen and don't offer explanations such as, 'Oh but I needed to go to . . .' Offer affirmations of feelings only: 'So I went there and you felt . . .' Explore with the child different times in their life they have felt this feeling and start to draw out common themes or underlying beliefs the child may be sharing. Do not ask your child, 'What do you believe will happen?', as they are unlikely to understand that question, but look for clues as to what they are connecting in these different examples. For instance, is the underlying belief: 'I am not safe when I am alone . . .' or: 'When Mummy goes out alone, something bad will happen to her . . .'? Keep in mind separation anxiety may not be focused on what is going to happen to them, but also to you. The child may be expressing a fear around you or another loved one being taken away from them.

Reflect

Gently find a way to re-enforce the message 'you will be safe'. Tread carefully with this, particularly if the child's anxiety relates to a real experienced previous trauma. It is no good saying 'that won't happen' when it already has. Do not minimise the event by saying, 'That is not likely to happen again,' either; allow space for the feelings that come up and focus on ways to minimise them happening again, rather than trying to change the past. Look for ways to help the child feel more in control, remembering that anxiety often comes from a belief of being at the mercy of something beyond one's control. Try to find any areas of control you can offer back to the child.

Acknowledge that this anxiety will not go away overnight and that it may take some time to work together. Remind them that you are always there, and even when you are not there, you are there 'in spirit'. I like to tell children that we are all connected by an invisible heart string and that no matter where in the world we are, the string can always find its owner and its loved ones. The string can help us communicate with each other when we are not together and the string can help us feel safe, when we might feel alone or scared.

'All the things you love are stored in your heart memory Wilbur, and nobody can ever change them or take them. Nothing that was special can ever be forgotten – a heart memory is a very safe place for keeping things.'

'In our new watering hole can I put more memories in my heart without forgetting my old ones?' asked Wilbur.

'Of course' laughed Mummy. 'An elephant never forgets, and a heart memory loves nothing more than having new ones to put inside.'

'I am very excited to put lots more things in my heart memory, Mummy.'

'Me too Wilbur', Mummy said.

From *Wilbur's Memory Box*

CHAPTER 7: BULLYING

GENDER DIFFERENCES IN BULLYING

Research shows that there are distinct differences in the ways males and females bully each other. Very early on in the social developmental of females, they are encouraged to socialise in groups of two, favouring 'special' or 'best' friends for interactions, whereas boys tend not to prioritise these individual friendships but look for group approval. Girls are socialised to be kind, and are encouraged to be a 'good friend', unlike boys who are told to be strong and 'active competitors', which will reward them with the group acceptance that they desire. These early differences in social development result in differences between how boys and girls bully.

Girls who have been socialised to appear kind and non-aggressive, in order to gain social approval, may resort to social exclusion tactics, name-calling or humiliation, rather than physical aggression. This type of bullying may even be masked as disgust or even concern for the victim, in order for the bully to maintain a 'nice girl' image. Social exclusion of other girls also allows for bullies to guard or protect friendships they consider as exclusive or special. This may take the form of 'divide and conquer' tactics, where one girl chooses to 'special friend' one girl for one week and reject her the next, which results in all the girls in the group flocking for this individual's attention lest she should be rejected, as that week's victim has been. This can appear to an outsider as simply an attempt by one girl to form close friendships with many and gain popularity but, in actual fact, it is a form of social dominance where she asserts herself as the alpha female.

This form of bullying is much more subtle and harder to interpret than outright name-calling or humiliation. Boys, on the other hand, attempt to maintain or gain social credibility through the physical domination of another, so they might resort to tactics such as physical harm or threats. This can be detected by others fairly obviously, but like the 'special friending' tactic of girls, boys may also use more subtle forms of dominance, such as humiliating behaviour disguised as 'jokes' or 'banter'. These may be done to appear harmless, and with the intention of getting a laugh from the group. But it is essentially the destruction of another's social standing within the hierarchy, in order to elevate or protect one's own.

All of these forms of bullying can be as harmful or damaging as each other, but it is important to note the differences and to understand the aim of each: social acceptance of a group, through the expulsion or domination of another.

'SUGAR AND SPICE AND ALL THINGS NICE.' WHAT CAUSES GIRLS TO BULLY?

If we return to the research on the differences in the ways the genders are socialised, we can see that the desire of the 'mean girl' is to achieve some sense of social superiority over others. Females are often told that physical beauty and popularity is the ultimate prize and therefore they may seek to hurt those who threaten their ideals in this respect. This is sometimes thought of as jealousy. It is important to note the difference between envy and jealousy: psychoanalytic theory tells us that envy is the wish to 'become another'. This is where we may see copycatting, or obsessional behaviour; jealousy is the wish to destroy another.

Here is where we may find the roots of bullying – the impulse to tear down another's social standing through critiquing their dress sense, physical appearance, social behaviour or personality. Both envy and jealousy can come from low self-esteem, but jealousy can be far more destructive to the child. A jealous girl may indeed resort to bullying. A girl who is masking other feelings of inadequacy or the fear of social rejection may also bully; she may not feel directly jealous of another – or be cognisant of feeling so – but she may fear that if she does not bully another and assert dominance (thus achieving social status) she will be marked as being socially inferior and she will 'be exposed'.

'BOYS WILL BE BOYS.' WHAT CAUSES BOYS TO BULLY?

Returning to the idea that boys fear garnering the negative attention of the 'pack', we can imagine how it can happen that they attempt to mark another as the 'weak' one. We see in the animal kingdom that some species will literally fight the weakest male to the death, or will exile him from the pack. Boys are trained from a young age to be acutely aware of the danger of standing out from the pack and pack hierarchy; the alpha male in a pack holds power and dominance and can be cruel or benevolent in his leadership. Boys therefore will fight to become the alpha or as close to the alpha (in order not to exact punishment) as possible. This means they may attempt to harm or exile the weakest members of the pack, as pack species do in the animal kingdom.

There is a more subtle form of male bullying that is masked, similarly to 'mean girl' behaviour, as friendly or joking, known as bantering. This form of bullying is hard for the victim to stand up to, as boys are encouraged to be thick skinned, to not show shame or upset, and to always take a joke – if they do not, they risk rejection from the group and possibly more outright forms of bullying, such as physical harm or complete rejection. A boy who fears his place in the social structure is under threat (similarly to girls who fear being 'exposed' for being inadequate or weak in some way) may also bully others, for fear of being challenged himself.

THE ISSUE OF BULLYING IN NEURODIVERSE POPULATIONS

A recent survey done by the charity Ambitious about Autism's youth council (2023) suggested that 75 per cent of children with ASC have experienced bullying. Equally children with ADHD and ODD (oppositional defiant disorder) have a higher risk of being bullied or becoming a bully than neurotypical children. As the nature of this condition means that the child is prone to interrupting, socially inappropriate behaviours and emotional outburst, this can make them the target for bullying.

Both ASC and ADHD can mean that a child does not read social cues particularly well and may find that their social behaviour is poorly received by others, but they don't understand why. This can lead to feelings of shame or rejection. Conversely, these children can also find themselves being encouraged into the class-clown or class-rebel type behaviours, whereby their behaviour is being used by others as a way to get a laugh or score a point. A neurodiverse child does not always understand the impact of their behaviour or their choices and may relish being the 'naughty' or the 'funny' one, as it creates friendships and connections. Neurodiverse children often struggle with gaining and maintaining friendships due to their emotional responses and impulsive behaviour, and may look for any opportunity for social connection, no matter how risky or inappropriate.

ADHD children can also develop bullying behaviours; this can be as a result of their poor stress response control, and also a desire to 'act up' in front of others. They will likely not view their behaviour as bullying at the time of the event, but as a necessary reaction to someone else's action.

ODD children, by nature of their condition, can bully others.

But their condition can also make them the target for bullying behaviour from authority figures who find the child's hostile manner unbearable. Just because a child is behaving in a manner that is inappropriate or aggressive, does not give an adult the right to attempt to scare or humiliate them. Parents with ODD children are often faced with this dilemma – behavioural management vs authoritarian control. ODD children have an extraordinary ability to never back down in a fight, and I often remind parents that to engage in combat with a child with ODD is to allow them the upper hand – if you have come to fight, you have come to the right place. Combative means of communication is the ODD child's comfortable place, and they will very likely never back down no matter the threat or risk to them. This can be a recipe for disaster in environments such as school.

The underlying thread with neurodiversity and bullying is shame. Shame about being different, shame about being perceived as socially impaired or out of control, and shame about their sometimes very literal isolation from others. The child sitting outside the headteacher's office, or being dragged out of the classroom by a teacher, is very often neurodiverse, and when these instances happen, their brain stores the message: people don't want to be around me, I am difficult to get on with.

Some neurodiverse children carry very difficult memories of being viewed as weird or abnormal; the things other people seem to find easy they find more challenging and they recognise early on in life that society doesn't 'do' challenging. Very few neurodiverse children actually have the ability to articulate what is overwhelming or distressing them so they attempt to communicate this in inappropriate ways such as emotional outburst or they attempt to mask it by 'stimming' – engaging in behaviours that calm them down, such as repetitive movements or speech patterns or explosive physical movements. Sadly, these attempts to calm and ground are often also met with a lack of understanding by others, and the cycle of social isolation and shame continues.

How to talk to your neurodiverse child about bullying

- Your neurodiverse child will not necessarily interpret the behaviour of others or themselves as bullying, so encourage them to talk to you about who they are playing with at school, and what they enjoyed about their day and what they didn't.
- Remember the connection of shame and neurodiversity – your child may very well believe they have caused the bullying as a result of their 'poor' behaviour, so tread carefully when broaching the subject.
- A neurodiverse child likely has a different idea to a neurotypical child of what is fair and what is right; this can often be the cause of disputes and distress. Discuss with your child the concept of turn-taking and sharing at an early age and role-play examples whereby they get a chance to manage their stress responses in these situations. Explain to them that fairness does not always mean 'everyone gets the same', and in some cases people need different things or approaches to get to the same place, so if they see someone getting different treatment to them, it might be because that person needs it.
- There is no shame in asking for help if YOU need something a little different in order to feel comfortable

and safe. Here is where educating them about their triggers really empowers children to ask for their needs to be met, prior to experiencing a meltdown or shutdown.

- Remind children that kindness should apply to everyone, and just as they are expected to be kind to others, they should expect others to be kind to them. So, if someone is doing something that makes them feel humiliated or small, this is likely not a kind behaviour and is not OK.

- Remind children that even if they are not sure if the behaviour was bullying, if it made them feel shame then it was not OK. If they are not sure what the cause or reason was for the behaviour, they can always discuss it with you or a trusted adult to check it out.

- Role-play scenarios with your child where you practise assertiveness. Offer simple examples, such as saying: 'I don't like that, stop it,' or: 'No.' If your child needs phrases where they need to be more direct, possibly in response to threatening or nasty behaviour, you can encourage phrases such as, 'You don't get to do that to me,' or, 'You won't do that to me.'

- Role-play with your child ways to articulate their sensory difficulties, such as 'I don't want to do that', 'I find that difficult' or 'I would like to do something else'.

- Help your child to articulate emotions and inner states by naming emotions such as anger, fear or shame. This is particularly key for ASC children who will likely find this very challenging.

HOW CAN WE RECOGNISE BULLYING?

We all know that talking to our children is important, and many parents will understand the need to be aware of their child's social media activity. But these more subtle forms of bullying such as girls singling out others for one week for special attention and rejecting them the next, or spreading malicious gossip, may be harder to detect. Similarly with banter between boys – when one boy is the constant object of the banter, it may be time to look more closely at how healthy these social structures are.

Signs to look out for that MIGHT suggest your child is being bullied

- Not wanting to go to school
- Feeling sick more often (particularly stomach complaints)
- Your child's things going missing regularly or are being destroyed
- Unexplainable injuries
- Sudden loss of friends or avoidance of school situations
- Receiving fewer invites for parties or play dates
- Sudden decline in child's mental health
- Decline in confidence or sudden onset of shyness
- Changes in eating patterns
- Academic decline
- Child wanting to change route to school or appears fearful of going to school
- 'Faking' illness
- Sudden onset of aggression or irritability at home

All of the above could be explained by things other than

bullying, but if many of these things occur it is possible your child is being bullied.

WAYS TO ASK YOUR CHILD ABOUT BULLYING

Your child might be extremely fearful or ashamed to admit to bullying, so it is never a good idea to ask outright: 'Are you being bullied?' Given that bullying often occurs within friendship groups, your child might not immediately identify the behaviour as bullying, and they may need help to frame it in this way – children who are often scapegoated by social groups will explain bullying away as just banter among friends. The impact to their self-esteem is nonetheless as damaging if the child terms it bullying or not.

General questions to ask:

- Who are you hanging out with lately? Tell me about them.
- What was the best thing that happened today? What was the worst?

If your child isn't sure it was bullying:

- Where did this happen?
- What was going on right before?
- Does this person who did this to you do this to anyone else?
- What do you think they were trying to do or show?

TEACHING 'SHAME SIGNALS'

If your child is unclear about a behaviour and whether it is bullying or not, a great tool we can use is to talk to our child about 'shame signals'. We can talk with our children about identifying behaviours in others that make them feel shame, that causing another person to feel hurt is NEVER banter, it is bullying. Shame is an emotion that tells us that we are unworthy in some way. Unlike guilt, where you can apologise for DOING something wrong, shame tells you that you must apologise as YOU are wrong. Shame is an emotion that is often triggered in one of four situations: unrequited love (such as when a child feels unlovable by the parent), disappointed expectations of self (such as feeling a failure in relation to an unachieved goal), exclusion, or unwanted exposure. The last two are the most common types of shame that we see used by bullies.

The bully will make the victim feel unwanted or an outsider, and this will in turn make the victim feel shame. Or they will expose a trait or difference about the victim that excludes them from the group, or makes them appear undesirable to the group.

Shame is not always easy to identify and sometimes we will identify it as guilt or embarrassment, but we can start even with young children to notice how their body responds to somebody's actions, and see if they are feeling any shame signals.

Shame is feeling:

- Small or humiliated
- Like wanting to run away
- Hot or nauseous
- Worried what others are thinking of you
- Disgusting or unlovable

- Frozen or lost for words
- Like wanting to cry, or crying

Teaching children about shame helps them to identify that when they feel this, they feel it in response to another's behaviour, and this is not acceptable. WE can further teach them that friends or not, they have every right to voice this and to express the wish for behaviour that doesn't cause them shame. We can inform our children that good friends do not attempt to shame another, as shame is a feeling that hurts not only one's feelings but one's soul; it tells us that we are unlovable / defective / worthless. Friends should never make us feel these things, even as a 'joke'. Shaming someone is never acceptable.

By getting children to focus exclusively on the emotion of shame we can help them identify toxic behaviours. It is important to remember the difference here between guilt and shame; with guilt you can apologise for something you have done wrong, shame is the belief that YOU are wrong. Bullying often has its basis in shame, and it is essential that children learn to identify early signs of shame in order to identify bullying. Many behaviours may cause us anger or distress, and these may not necessarily be bullying. If someone is attempting to shame you they are not being a kind friend. Someone on the other hand may be trying to guilt you as they are pointing out what you have done wrong to them; this is not necessarily a poor friend and we can explain this to children by saying, 'Are they making you feel bad for what you did or for being you?'

TALKING TO YOUR CHILD ABOUT IDENTIFYING BULLYING

Talking to your child about bullying may bring up a lot of emotions for you — anger, sadness, maybe even a trigger of your own shame, but unfortunately as many of us learnt while we were at school, bullying happens. Our role as parents is to be listeners and responders; we do not simply tell our child to 'toughen up' or, 'If someone hits you, you hit them back,' just because that's what our parents told us. Both of those responses minimise the bullying and are rejecting the child's appeal for help. As we now know, that attachment is formed by the idea of parent = safe space; we do not ever want our child to feel that if they come to us they will be brushed aside. So how do we have conversations about bullying with our children?

We have discussed the importance of teaching children to identify shame signals in order for them to understand what that feels and looks like. This can be particularly helpful to assist children with identifying bullying behaviours if they are unsure what is happening. In some instances, however, this is unnecessary and your child has already identified they have been the subject of bullying, so what do you do?

Extract–Express–Reflect for bullying

Time, Tone, Temper (see page 94) is your best friend here. Be mindful of how the information about your child being bullied came to light — did they tell you? Did someone else? This will be key in determining how to choose your setting and your time. If your child tells you, they have chosen the time and space, so go with that. If someone else has told you, choose a time whereby your child will feel they have privacy and security to open up. Ask them, 'May I talk to you?', and explain in clear and non-emotive language what you would like to share.

Extract

Remain calm, be mindful that your reaction can invoke shame in your child. When we appear shocked or horrified your child can interpret this as a reminder to them how horrified they should be in relation to this event. Be calm, be kind. Use words like, 'It's safe to tell me', 'I am here to protect you . . .', 'Just tell me as much as you can, I am here to listen . . .' Open the floor for whatever they want to share, and do not interrupt. Do not ask questions such as, 'Did you not do / did you think to / why didn't you?' This can make the child feel even more at fault and shamed; simply remind your child they are loveable, loving and loved. You are there to protect them, and you have no agenda beyond that.

Express

Do not minimise what has been shared by your child by saying, 'Maybe it wasn't that bad.' Adults often have a tendency to minimise childhood bullying as we do it in order to protect our own inner child from remembering the shame of feeling excluded or bullied by another child. You can often see adults saying things such as, 'Well that's just kids . . .' or, 'Kids can be mean', in order to block the shame they might feel as a result of their own difficult childhood experiences, or the shame of feeling the parent of the bullied child. If this is you, do some work on your own feelings of shame BEFORE approaching your child. People who feel shame often think of alternative narratives that seek to block their shame, so when we as parents try to offer too many reasons why it probably wasn't 'that bad', we run the risk of furthering shaming, by devaluing the experience. Instead, say things like, 'I can see why you felt that.'

Be wary of sharing your own experiences, and only do this if it is consented to by your child. Say, 'I think I have had something similar – may I tell you about it?' rather than, 'That happened to me.' For some children, hearing your experiences may make them feel heard and seen but for others they may be too stuck in their own shame to hear about anyone else's, and they may become resentful or feel you are not listening. Offer the example and back off immediately if your child reacts defensively or dismissively.

Reflect

Think together about next steps. Telling the school – should we do this together or would you like me to? Should we discuss with the other child's parents? Do not push your own agenda here, let them take back control and dictate the outcome. Ask your child, 'What would make you feel safe now?' and listen to their answer!

Don't be afraid to ask direct questions: 'Do you want to go back there?' 'Do you want to change schools?' and – the next bit is going to be the tricky bit – be prepared to act if they say yes. For some parents this might seem the opposite of teaching a child resilience as it goes against the message of 'toughen up'. To those parents I would say: would you choose to return to an environment where you were being tormented every day if there was an alternative? Too often we ask children and teens to endure behaviour in others we would never tolerate in other adults. If your child tells you they want to change schools, take this seriously and tell them you will look into this option. This can help your child to see that you take them seriously, and that you are on their side.

If your child has informed you of something that is illegal, calmly explain to them that what they have just told you is very serious and you will be taking steps in order to protect them. Do not force the issue; if your child refuses, calmly discuss with them why they do not want to involve the police. The child in this instance is most likely scared, and is asking you to make them feel safe before they can agree to involve the police. Your child may also not understand the severity of the issue and needs you to explain why the behaviour they have disclosed is so dangerous and why it needs to be stopped. Discuss with your child how you will protect them following a disclosure to the police and be open to a discussion that involves moving schools if that is what the child wants.

Bullying, if ignored or allowed to persist, can have very extreme effects on a child's mental health, and in some cases it can be fatal. Take your child's account seriously and do not be afraid to take assertive action if you have any concerns about your child's safety or if they are expressing feelings of suicidality.

WHAT TO DO IF *YOUR* CHILD IS BULLYING SOMEONE

Hearing or suspecting that your child is bullying someone can be an extremely shameful and distressing experience for a parent. However, just as we don't react with 'our stuff' when our child tells us they are being bullied, we don't jump in feet first when we discover our child is the bully. Children who bully others often feel scared, angry or alone in some aspect of their life. Sit down and consider: has anything changed in your child's life recently – how did they react?

If the school contact you to tell you they have concerns about your child's behaviour in relation to another, do not jump to the defensive or say 'all kids bully'. Being told your child is bullying another is a possible sign that your child is suffering and is causing others to suffer as a result. Happy children do not bully others. It is of course possible that the narrative is incorrect and that your child has done nothing wrong, but calmly listen to the description of behaviour you are being offered. Do not immediately jump to an explanation of the behaviour.

Questions to ask school:

- So, what did you see?
- And what did my child do?
- What was happening before?
- Have they done this before?
- Are they normally friendly with this child?

Extract–Express–Reflect if your child is bullying someone

Extract

This is not going to be easy, but you must find a calm space to repeat to your child exactly what the school has said, and then wait and allow the space for them to absorb and respond. If they do not respond, offer them the invitation by saying, 'I would like to hear what you think, I am not going to interrupt.' Do not use the phrase 'your side of the story' – we are trying here to not set this discussion as a 'he said-she said'; we want to encourage an open dialogue. Re-read the section on Time, Tone, Temper (see page 94) if needed, as this is going to be vital to having a productive discussion.

Ask for the who, what, why and where. Do not let your child minimise what has happened or what they did. Keep asking for the facts in a non-judgemental way, but make it clear that you are after facts rather than an 'alibi'. A very important question in this stage of the process is why THAT child; listening carefully to this answer might give you some vital clues on why your child is engaging in this behaviour. For example, is it envy on your child's part? Is it the need to impress? Is it being scared of being the victim?

Express

Use empathy-based questions such as, 'Do you find that funny? Do you think they thought that was funny? How do you know that?' Ask for your child's reflections on the relationship they had had with this child and how the other child might perceive that relationship. Ask your child to consider how they would feel in this other child's shoes.

Reflect

Remind your child that you love them and you are here to help, but bullying is not a behaviour you will condone. Return to the reasons you might suspect your child has for behaving in this way (jealousy, anxiety about fitting in, fear of other bullies) and acknowledge them kindly and honestly. Do not, however, allow them to be used as a justification for bullying. I always use the phrase in my house that 'anger is allowed but aggression is not' – there may be many valid self-esteem-based reasons your child has for bullying someone, but it does not mean that the behaviour should be condoned or allowed to continue. Be clear with your child that you are there to help them with their feelings, but bullying will not be tolerated, ever.

HOW DO WE TEACH OUR CHILDREN TO BE INCLUSIVE?

One of the best ways to create healthy, compassionate spaces within classrooms and friendship groups is to teach children from a young age to be inclusive. When we don't celebrate differences in others and when we model behaviour that separates ourselves from others, children learn this as a tool to go forward with in their own life. When we can teach children that the world can appreciate differences in others and be kind to those who wish to live differently to us, we teach them that social exclusion is never necessary. Children will of course have preferences for friends and for those whom they wish to spend time with – this is OK! You have those preferences as an adult, and so do they, but they do not need to see others who don't share their views or interests as inferior to them or not deserving of their respect – this is where ideas around bullying can grow.

TIPS FOR RAISING CHILDREN WHO CELEBRATE OTHERS

1. **Saying no to groups that 'exclude'**
    While creating in-groups and out-groups is part of human nature to some extent, we should encourage our children to avoid playing in groups that actively seek to

exclude or include certain people. I hate to say it, but I see this type of behaviour in the playground among parents, where certain children are chosen for certain things, or some children are consistently left off invite lists. Social exclusion is also the most common form of bullying and the least likely to be taken seriously by adults. Teach your child that choosing a 'common enemy' is neither kind nor productive. When we mark people as 'not our tribe' we may miss the opportunity to engage with people who could teach us new things, who could expand our horizons and become a great friend.

2. **Model inclusion**
   Look honestly at your own family and social structure – how often are you exposed to people who are different from you? In what way could you change this? Also consider your own beliefs and stereotypes – are you teaching your children through your language and your actions that certain groups of people are inferior to you or carry negative messages? If we want to raise inclusive children, we have to model inclusive attitudes within our home.

3. **Support individuality**
   Encourage your children to value not only themselves as unique and worthwhile people, but others as well. Encourage your child to view the world through the lens of curiosity and excitement. Remind them that if everyone was the same, the world would be a boring place.

4. **Prioritise values in people, rather than 'coolness'**
   When you teach your child to look at who someone is, rather than what clothes they wear or what they play

with, you automatically teach them to try to look beyond obvious social markers or connections – 'you look like me so we are alike' or 'you like what I like so we are alike' – and ask them to think about the values they would like to have in a friend.

5. **Be an includer**

Encourage your child to reach out to new children, or to sit next to the child who is often left out or forgotten about. A great tool is to ask your child to find out one interesting fact about the child they often complain about; by doing this they are learning that everyone has something to offer, and everyone is valuable.

6. **Promote diverse friendships**

Research has shown that kids who have a diverse set of friendships will not only be more accepting of others, but they are also less likely to be bullied. Why is this? Because they have learnt to adapt to different environments and different types of people. When you can teach a child that difference doesn't have to be a barrier, you open up their world to greater possibilities, and greater likelihood of them finding a place where they can 'belong'.

7. **Taking a break from a difficult friendship**

Sometimes we need to support our child in the decision to take a step back from a friendship where they are feeling hurt or bullied. Children often need some guidance around how to set boundaries confidently and assertively and you can encourage them to say, 'I don't like that and I am going to need to take some space.' It is a very important tool to teach a child how to create distance with respect and that by setting boundaries with others it doesn't mean they can never be friends with that person again. You remind them that they can re-engage in the friendship when the person treats them with respect.

8. **Stand up for others**

One of the best things you can teach your child that will actually help not only your child but the environment around them is to teach them to stand up for others. Research shows that bullying cultures can be stopped when one person takes a stand against it. Empower your child to speak out against bullying, either directly to the bullies, or to tell a teacher or an adult if they feel safer to do this. Standing up for others can also come in the form of what you do rather than what you say, so choosing to sit with the excluded child or inviting them to play can be a powerful anti-bullying message that can help make the environment of everyone a much happier place.

Activities for helping to teach inclusion

The wrinkled heart activity

This can be a great one to do with a group of children but it can also be done individually. Very simply, ask your child to cut a heart shape out of paper.

Then scrunch it up. Ask the child to smooth it out. Explain that means that words 'leave wrinkles on a heart' and even if we try to smooth them out the heart feels a wrinkle from those words. Think before you cause a wrinkle!

The toothpaste

Similar to the wrinkled heart, ask your child to squeeze a stripe of toothpaste on to a surface and then ask them to get it back in the tube. Remind them that what we say and what we do cannot be undone: be selective in what we say.

THINK strategy

Teach your child to THINK before they speak, write or type. Is what I am about to say:

> True?
> Helpful?
> Important?
> Necessary?
> Kind?

Teaching children to communicate in this way helps them to understand mindful communication, and to show tact and compassion in their words.

CHAPTER 8: FAILURE

One of my heroes is Brené Brown who, among the many inspiring things she says from her lifelong study of vulnerability, describes vulnerability as 'the birthplace of innovation, creativity and change'. Let's process that for a second: by being vulnerable, by opening ourselves up to failure, criticism, embarrassment, we create a space where ideas grow. Dr Brown puts this far more eloquently than I can when she says that 'vulnerability is not winning or losing, it's having the courage to show up when you can't control the outcome'. As a child therapist I sit back in awe of this quote and imagine a world where we told children that the only critics worth listening to are those who want to drive you on; those who want to offer advice rather than shut you down. Or a world where we tell children that when we fail, we simply pass another stage of a creative process.

All children are artists, the problem is to remain an artist as we grow up: not my words, but taken from Picasso, who I imagine knew a little bit about being a creative genius. Sir Ken

Robinson, in his wonderful, celebrated TED Talk, also pointed out the sad fact that most children don't remain 'artists', as we tell them at a young age they won't get a job being one. But when we do that, we kill all that creativity, passion and fire, simply because someone might not want to buy it one day. We effectively teach children that the only thing 'worthy' about you is that which you can exchange for external reward. We remove all the messaging about intrinsic self-worth and motivation and – most importantly – joy! When we tell children not to enjoy the process of making, breaking and creating we tell them we are only interested in the finished product; we don't want to hear about how you got there.

So let's stop telling children that everything has to be right, and if not it's wrong. Let's stop telling them that some subjects or pursuits are not worthy, or some are more worthy than others. Let's start leading by example and showing the courage to embrace our own creativity; show your children that you have interests and passions that you nurture simply because they feel wonderful. Show your children that you are willing to try something you may not be 'good at', show them that mastery takes practice, and in that practice comes failure, maybe even embarrassment, but this is simply the 'sample testing' stage of product design. If you run a business, show your staff that mistakes can mean that you tried, and that the way to recover from them is not to blame others and cover your back for fear of recrimination, but to try again.

If we want to breed a generation of creative empaths, let's stop judging others for errors, let's show kindness and encouragement in the face of failure – our children will do the same. We don't need to teach them competition, we need to teach them collaboration: let's rebuild it, let's redesign it. I am going to leave you here with the words of Dr Brown, who always says what I want to say better than me: 'When we spend our lives waiting to be perfect before we walk into the arena, we squander our precious time and we turn our backs on our gifts and the unique contributions only we can make.'

FAILURE AND SCHOOL

I was speaking to a teacher who told me recently that 'our pastoral theme this year is grit'. Great, I said, and how are you teaching that? 'Well, you know, just don't give up when stuff gets hard . . . and er . . . you know, get through the exam season . . . and just keep going basically.' Ah, wonderful, I thought, the E word, the good old E word. As excited as I was to see the theme of grit being promoted, I was less than elated to see it applied as: let's use this wonderful idea as yet another 'methodology' to achieve high grades. Earlier in the book, I wrote about the modern mother sinking under a never-ending wave of messaging to be a perfect version of mothering, but our children are also sinking – under a never-ending wave of pressure to 'achieve'. I see with my own eyes more and more children coming to me talking about 'failing' when, in reality, they are describing any situation that is not perfect. I am not even referring to teens here – younger children are also getting swallowed up in this. The more our school systems test and examine for standardised scores, school places, scholarships and their own vanity of league tables, the more our children fall prey to that insidious message – 'My output is the measure of me.'

I have had a child tell me they 'know' they didn't do well in that school interview; that child was six. I have heard children

145

say, 'I don't have time to play, I have too much work to do'; those children were nine. And I have also heard, 'My teacher told me if I don't study for these GCSEs I'm going to work in McDonald's.' Let's just stop here: academic output is NOT a measure of success and it's definitely not the route to happiness, and, also, what's wrong with working in McDonald's? When are we going to stop telling children that the only thing they should aspire towards is a job? What about a contented life? Successful relationships? Happy homes? Our children have never faced more messaging about 'achievement' and 'success' – we need to help them understand that success is not necessarily a full bank account.

CHILDREN ARE INHERENTLY GOOD AT FAILING

Babies learn through failure all the time, and they are experts at understanding how to use failure as a learning tool. Watch a baby or toddler learning how to master a skill such as walking or grasping an object. While you may see anger or frustration cloud their tiny features, one thing you will never see is shame or embarrassment – why? Because a baby has no concept of the embarrassment of failure. No one tells the baby, 'You should be embarrassed for not being able to do this, or not getting it the first time.' The baby simply views this task as one that needs repeating in order to gain mastery of it; they do not bog themselves down with the negative social connotations of 'being a failure'. For this reason they are highly skilled at adapting and improving. This wonderful little brain is constantly thinking of new ways to tackle this problem, and taking a moment to actually consider the momentous task of learning not only to stand, but to walk, then to run, then to jump. This is years' worth of work – but they do not see the road ahead as one of crushing failure, they see this as simply a set of steps on a learning journey. Why? Because they do not start with the notion that not getting something the first time is a failure.

Children continue on this self-assured little path until they start to be conscious of other children and what they can do – this age of comparison usually happens at around four or five years old (no coincidence that for many children this is the age they start some type of formal education). So our wonderful self-confident little being starts to see that 'other people can do things better or worse than me'. Remember that children do not inherently consider themselves superior or inferior to others, they obtain this message by watching the reactions from the adults around them. We will never be able to prevent this comparison – it is a natural stage of brain development whereby the brain observes two actions or objects and analyses the differences between them. This is an important step of brain development; doing this helps our child to develop tools like risk assessment of situations and people, also to make choices between options or actions. We don't want to prevent children making comparisons, but we do want to LIMIT the impact of them when comparisons are being made about them in relation to others. So how do we do this?

- We don't speak in words of negative comparison in order to encourage change, so we NEVER say, 'Look at X and what they can do, you should try to copy them.'
- We remind children at all times of the benefits of diversity and difference. I often tell my children that 'every flower

is beautiful but no petal is the same'. In other words, our version of success may be very different to someone else's but all versions of success are worthy.

- We focus on celebrating EFFORT rather than output.

HOW TO TALK TO YOUR NEURODIVERSE CHILD ABOUT ACADEMIC CHALLENGES

No one needs to tell the parent of a neurodiverse child that school is going to throw up some significant challenges for your child and their self-esteem. It is often around early primary school that neurodivergent children start noticing they are 'different', and crucially it is around this same age they start to ingest the message, 'and that difference is not a good thing'. Parents of neurodiverse children can arm their child with self-confidence and self-acceptance by giving them the tools and, most importantly, the knowledge to understand their different brain, and why it is a wonderful thing!

- As with bullying, remind your child that to be neurodiverse is a wonderful thing but it comes with some differences and this might mean that they learn in a different way and at a different rate to others.
- If your child has dyslexia or dyspraxia alongside their other diagnoses, explain to them what this means and how these things are simply a sign of a different learning style.
- Ensure your child's teacher is armed with everything they need to know about your neurodiverse child in order to get the best from them academically.

- For ADHD children this can mean rest breaks, sitting at the front of the class, asking to repeat instructions back to them to ensure they have understood, offering extensions for longer pieces of work and understanding discrepancies in handwriting output vs verbal output, for example.
- If necessary, ask your child's school to involve the SEN department in creating classroom practices that are empirically proven to help support their particular type of neurodiversity.

NEGATIVE VS POSITIVE ENFORCEMENT

I often hear parenting advice given to only ever encourage and to never cajole. I agree with this . . . however, I am going to say something that some may find mildly controversial. I do think there is a place for the words, 'You are better than this.' Now, before you throw the book down and think – Alison have you lost your mind?! – let me explain.

As children grow up, and particularly around the primary school age, they can start to feel bogged down in negative beliefs of themselves or negative ideas about how well they think they will 'do'. This is particularly prevalent in children who may have had academic struggles or are neurodivergent, and what can happen with this group of children is the negative belief becomes entrenched and they start to think the bare minimum of effort is what is required. They fear that the act of trying to achieve a goal sets them up for the soul-crushing possibility of 'failure'. Therefore it is safer to stay a bare-minimum kinda kid. They might refuse homework or they might sit coasting in a class or set that is below their potential ability – again, why? Because they lack the self-confidence to put themselves into that highly vulnerable place of trying. Remember the Brené Brown quote earlier about the arena? They don't want to put themselves in the arena.

So this is where you as a parent can offer them a life-affirming message of, 'I believe in you.' These children, where school or life in general has given them one too many hard messages about the potential social embarrassment of failing, will not necessarily hear the words 'I believe in you', they will dissociate and glaze over – yeah, yeah Mum . . . Translation: I don't believe in me.

So now you step in with a more direct re-enforcement of 'You are better than this.' What these words do is jolt the child out of that haze of self-doubt and into a space where they have to ponder this thought in relation to themselves: am I better than this? Can I do more? You may get a negative, even combative response back of, 'No I am not, stop saying this stuff.' Great! You have got them to engage; you have inspired the fight they need to find in themselves to make a decision – is this what I am going to do? You have told them: 'I see you, you matter, and I believe in you even if you don't.'

This tactic only works if you truly believe the child is refusing or not attempting to 'try'. If the child is doing their all but YOU think they should or could do more, then you are knocking their confidence further. You must only ever use this tool when you know the child is actively avoiding a task or action; it must never be used to further your views of 'I want my child to be XYZ' – that is doing the opposite of what this intends.

THE BEST QUESTION YOU WILL EVER ASK

After using the 'you are better than this' approach, it is important that when the child decides to try again, the message is, 'You make yourself proud first before anybody else.' My daughter recently came to me with full marks on her spelling test; this was a wonderful achievement and she had worked so hard to get her goal of, 'Mummy, next week I want them all right.' She had told me crestfallen in the car a few weeks before: 'Mummy, I got 2 out of 10 like I always do on my spellings, again,' so I talked to her about this and we both agreed that actually the reason she had got this score was she hadn't been taking the time to learn them, and with every week she got the lowest score in the class, the more she felt like not attempting to learn them. She avoided them, she sometimes took them out of her bag and hid them. But having relieved herself of this story and the feeling of shame about getting the 'worst' score on the spelling test, we made a plan to work on next week's. The following week she got 6/10 and the next week . . . she got them all.

She came dancing out of school shouting about her results and I filled with tears watching how happy she felt. She laughed and said:

Mummy are you crying because you are so proud?
Always Issy, but more importantly: are you proud of you?
Yes.
Then nothing in this world is more important than that. I am proud of you every day, you never need to work for that, but our brains can trick us into not feeling proud of ourselves, so if you can end this day saying I am proud of me, that's work well done.

Every time your child asks: 'Are you proud of me?', re-enforce that your pride in them never falters, but the only person they have to make proud in this world is themselves. When you remind them of this message you embed the idea that self-worth comes from self-love, and self-motivation comes from self-worth. If your child comes to you and says, 'Mummy, I love you, but I don't care what you think of me', pat yourself on the back: you have raised a self-confident, healthy and securely attached little being.

Get comfortable with your own ideas about failure, particularly academic failure.

If you have been following this book up until this point, you will be aware that I have fairly strong views on getting a handle on your own psychological 'stuff' as a parent, in order not to pass it on to your child. Never is this more important than in relation to academic or even sporting success. I rarely see a more triggered parent than one who is facing parent–teacher night or, even worse, exam results day. Our own school days may plague us or delight us with the memories contained therein, and we may pat ourselves on the back or metaphorically beat ourselves up for what we did or didn't do at school. That's fine, but your child is not you, their school is not yours (even if it was!) and their life roadmap is not yours to manage. Keep your own hang-ups about school or teachers in check, or you will not be able to support your child in their academic journey. Remember our mantra: 'You are not the owner of your child.' Their life is not a representation of you. Resist the urge to make this about you or the failure or success of your parenting; this is particularly challenging in an academic environment that seems designed to pit people against each other, and can easily descend into a competition of who is the better parent (in other words, whose child got the better grades). Rise above this by reminding yourself that by making this about you, you are no longer making it about your child.

'FAILURE' IN TERMS OF BEAUTY: A SIDE NOTE FOR PARENTS OF GIRLS

Anybody who knows me will you tell the hill I die upon will be engraved with the words: 'Being beautiful is the least interesting thing about you.' Let me tell you why. Girls are told from a frighteningly young age that the most important thing they can be is beautiful. Messages around female beauty start from babyhood – in the same way messages around male strength and 'capability' start from babyhood. We tell our girls that in order to be viewed as an achiever, the world must view them as aesthetically pleasing. To be viewed as 'un-pretty' is to be viewed as a failure. This is psychologically damaging on a number of levels.

One of the things I am most conscious of as a mother of daughters is the messaging they receive from media and TV about physical appearance, and as a result I choose to heavily censor what I feel is inappropriate messaging about being pretty as something we should all aspire to. Why? Because while I know society is going to badger them with this message for most of their life, I want them to at least have the chance to develop a strong enough foundation to withstand that maelstrom. To put this into context, recently two friends of mine told me their daughters were concerned that they 'looked fat'. They are six years old.

Some people might think this is all a storm in a teacup

and little girls have always played with dolls, and loved 'pretty princesses'. What's the issue? The issue is that we have moved so far beyond simply the enjoyment of playing with dolls or listening to stories about princesses that we are living in an age where pre-teens are social media stars, where primary school age children are 'influencers', where advertising agencies are deliberately marketing cosmetics / bikinis with padded bras and dolls who 'need to fix their face'. What is the real life and very sobering impact of this media barrage? A widespread mental health epidemic in teenage girls the like of which society has never seen. A recent study by the NHS (Mental health of young people and children: 2023) said that record numbers of girls under 15 are accessing NHS mental health services, and that the gap between mental issues in girls and boys has never been bigger. Girls were 30 per cent more likely to suffer from mental issues at the age of 11 than boys, and by the time they reach 18 that figure doubles. Girls are also four times more likely to suffer from an eating disorder, and 77.5 per cent of young women aged 17 to 19 were likely to have 'problems with eating' as defined by the study. There could be many reasons for this, but with 61 per cent of 10–17-year-old girls reporting low self-esteem according to a research study by Dove (Self Esteem Project: 2022), and 1 in 2 of them relating this to images of perfection on social media, I think it is fair to interpret that the messages around body image and self-worth are a connection. Particularly when we look at the statistic that advertisers are twice as likely to promote 'aspirational images of beauty' to sell their products to girls as they are to boys.

So, parents of girls, join me in reminding your daughters that 'being beautiful is the least interesting about you' with these tips!

1. **Watch your language**

   Children learn by demonstration, so watch your choice of language and tone when describing yourself or other women. Do not discuss your weight or the weight of other women in front of your young daughters; where possible, compliment a non-physical attribute in other women. For example, you could remark on the dedication of an athlete, the talent of an actress, or the eloquence of an activist rather than their appearance.

2. **Celebrate your daughter's talents / gifts / strengths**

   The rest of society will go out of their way to tell your daughter she is beautiful or cute or a 'princess' – you don't need to feed into that. Celebrate your daughter's kindness, her strength, her bravery, her resilience. Offer constant reminders of all the things she is, aside from her physical appearance.

3. **No this doesn't mean never compliment your daughter!**

   Of course it is OK to tell your daughter she is beautiful as long as there is EQUAL or GREATER focus on all the other things she is, aside from this. The key here is to remind your daughter that 'beauty is the least interesting thing about you'.

4. **Find activities that don't fit female stereotypes**

   Give the ballet class, the piano lesson, the acting class a rest for a bit and try something that puts no emphasis on appearance: try skateboarding, try football, try martial arts. There is nothing wrong with activities that celebrate performance or beauty, but balance them out with activities that place no value on these things.

5. **Get outside and climb some trees**

   Encourage your daughter's sense of adventure, encourage her to feel curious about the world and get her hands muddy. Being in nature and exploring the world around you is a fantastic way to help your daughter discover interests, promote creativity and develop imagination.

6. **Get creative!**

   Find ways to help your daughter embrace her creativity, art / music / cooking / pottery. Anything that involves creative expression has been shown to increase serotonin, the happy chemical, and to boost self-confidence.

7. **Monitor her media consumption**

   This is huge: ensure that what comes into your house is healthy, positive and empowering. You will not be able to control everything your daughter sees and hears, but you do have control over what is consumed in your house. Check TV programmes or reading material before your child watches them to ensure they contain messaging that you would wish to promote, and the same goes for any kind of social media. Filtering what your daughter absorbs in your home where she is safe and loved will do a huge amount to combat the messaging she hears from outside of it.

8. **Find positive role models**

   These don't have to be famous, they can be fictional or even someone you know. Find female role models who are inspirational or admirable for something other than their appearance.

PARENTS OF BOYS – CHALLENGING THE 'STRONG MAN' STEREOTYPE!

I am the aunt of two wonderful little boys, and in the same way I see my girls bombarded with messages about beauty and femininity, I watch with a similar sense of dread, the media messages my beloved nephews are given about male strength. Boys' toys are marketed at the message 'men need to be strong' and 'strong men have muscles'. There has been a huge amount of discussion already about negative correlations of strength-dominance and the impact on male psychological development, and it is so encouraging that this discourse is being had, in the media and in homes. But I would like to flag another trend that I think has been under-recognised in younger males – male strength and the desire for a muscular aesthetic. A recent survey (YouGov: 2019) found that 28 per cent of young men have felt anxious about their body image, and 11 per cent of the surveyed participants had suicidal thoughts as a result of their body image.

In a survey conducted with 13- and 14-year-olds (Bereal: 2018), 26 per cent of boys said that social media caused them to worry about their body – specifically the desire to be tall and muscular. This becomes extremely concerning when 10 per cent who were surveyed said that they would consider taking steroids to achieve this ideal. I have seen through my own clinic and the work of my colleagues that the number of boys and young men seeking treatment for eating disorders has exponentially grown over the last few years. The mental health of children and young people in the UK survey (2023) showed that 40 per cent of boys surveyed describe eating patterns that could be considered disordered; these figures reflect the even more concerning trend that eating disorder diagnoses in boys has doubled since 2020.

So what do we do about it?

Let's start by asking ourselves – how often do we actively monitor the images boys consume in relation to male aesthetics? How often do we feel free to discuss weight and body images in front of boys in a way we might possibly be more wary of doing in front of girls? Note the toys your son plays with – what body images are pervasive? What celebrities does your son like and what body image do they have?

When I asked myself the above questions in relation to my nephews, I realised that almost every male they admire has an athletic physique, and not once had I considered what these images might be doing. We don't often hear boys, for example, describe their toys or the characters they like in celebration of their looks, in the same way we hear girls describe things as 'pretty' but it would be naïve to suggest that the consistency of these muscular images is not imprinting themselves on boys' brains as the 'ideal'. When we consider this subtle marketing of toys as muscular and strong and then look back at the figures of boys' body image issues, maybe we have all missed something in our understanding of male development. Boys are also susceptible to body image concerns, not simply as teens from social media consumption, but much earlier – from the images they see as children.

So, parents of boys – look at the tips above I have shared for girls and think how many of these you can start applying to your sons. Let's start promoting the message that male bodies can also come in all shapes and sizes, and that to be muscular is not the goal. In other words, 'to be physically perfect is the least interesting thing about you'.

Extract–Express–Reflect for failure

Extract

What is the child telling you that has made them feel a failure? Don't skip over the details here; sometimes it might not be what happened but the reaction to what happened. Ask questions like, who was there? What did they do? Get context like time of day, energy levels and previous preparation. This is important context as we can use some of this in our reflect section. For example, if your child felt a failure at the end of a long, hard day when they were tired, use this reflection to remind them, 'Darling, maybe this is your body being tired, not your brain / body being a failure.' Getting context is always important as it helps us to gather later information that might be a reflection point.

Express

What did they feel about the event and, most importantly, what did they feel about themselves? Listen patiently and offer descriptive language to help your child articulate their feelings. Young children may not always be able to name feelings, so get them to describe the body sensation and the thoughts that go with it, then offer an emotion. If they name an emotion, go with that.

Don't forget to focus on the reactions as well as the event, as very often shame comes from the reaction of other people. Think back to the baby example: a baby doesn't feel embarrassment for falling over, as they do not have the emotional literacy to read others' emotions and nor do they understand the message that 'failure is embarrassing'. Your verbally articulate child has both of these things and they very likely have imbibed the message 'I have failed and that's a bad thing' down to the reaction (or perceived reaction!) of others rather than the event itself. Did anyone make them feel small or silly as a result of this? Did anyone say anything that made them uncomfortable?

Reflect

Using all of the contextual details you have gathered, help your child to form a narrative of 'I can try again', and also 'failure is just a step in a process'. If your child is describing a sense of failure for something inherent about them such as being neurodivergent or their appearance, re-enforce the message that this is neither something to apologise for or be embarrassed of – we are all different and that is a wonderful thing! If, however, they are discussing an act or action that could be repeated, look for ways to identify possible setbacks (lack of preparation, timing etc.) and ways to readdress them in the future. Then above all find a narrative that celebrates the effort and achievement they have already made, as with any time we use this technique, we focus on giving the child a sense of agency and pride. Remind them of all the ways they helped themselves, and even, if appropriate, the people who helped them.

Look for a narrative that gives the child a positive message as opposed to one of self-condemnation or negative beliefs about the world.

CHAPTER 9: SIBLING RIVALRY

Family therapy focuses on the idea that families work dynamically with each other – they will often attempt to pull apart from each other to carve out emotional independence, but they will also draw back together to work as a dynamic team. We learnt earlier about how the dynamic between parents can contribute to the family dynamic and about the importance of modelling healthy conflict, but what about the dynamic between siblings? Let's return to Bowen's theory of family systems (see page 62) to learn a little bit more about how sibling position and birth order can impact personality.

SIBLING POSITION

There is no more classic triangle than that of siblings and parent. Sibling rivalry is the ultimate example of triangulation – two competing forces vying for alignment with a third. We also see, in larger families, siblings forming allegiances with each other to exclude another; sometimes they may do this to exclude a parent. Triangles can be formed within families many times over, and a family of four can be in up to ten triangles at any one time!

The below table lays out Bowen's thoughts on what birth order actually means for your personality development and your place in the triangle system. Without too much judgement, try to find your own birth position and its corresponding label and see how closely you think it fits you. Now consider that of your parents and also their parents: can you see any links?

Bowen's Sibling Positions

1. **Oldest brother of brothers**
   Characteristics: responsibility, loyalty
2. **Youngest brother of brothers**
   Characteristics: spontaneous, being 'one of the gang'
3. **Oldest brother of sisters**
   Characteristics: gets along well with women, charming
4. **Youngest brother of sisters**
   Characteristics: often chosen as the leader, maybe babied or favoured within the family
5. **Male only child**
   Characteristics: values responsibility and can be a perfectionist; self-confident and gets along well with

those older than him

6. **Twins**

   Characteristics: a life entwined with each other but this can create both extreme closeness and extreme competitiveness

7. **Oldest sister of sisters**

   Characteristics: likes to be in charge, brave, self-sacrificing

8. **Youngest sister of sisters**

   Characteristics: competitive, creative, a risk taker

9. **Oldest sister of brothers**

   Characteristics: maternal, independent

10. **Youngest sister of brothers**

    Characteristics: a social butterfly, feminine, collaborative

11. **Female only child**

    Characteristics: close to mother, can be people pleasing, self-confident

12. **Middle siblings**

    Characteristics: may play multiple roles depending on gender balance of family, can often find themselves as the peacemaker

Bearing in mind these are only Bowen's suggested interpretations, consider how you felt finding your own, and your other family members' corresponding birth order positions. What does this tell you?

Now consider that of your partner, or ex-partners – what does theirs tell you about them and the dynamic that you create together?

THE 'ROLE' OF BIRTH ORDER

Family systems theory tells us that in each family the child will be given a role; this role will enable the system to function and survive, even if the role is not a particularly pleasant one. The reason for this is that family systems theory supports the idea that families attempt to create harmony and reduce friction, and they do this by asserting subtle roles or characteristics on each individual in order to 'give everyone a job'. That job might be to keep the peace, to ask the difficult questions, to bring the humour, or to take a lead role. Let's have a quick look at some of the roles we commonly see children playing in their family system.

The Mediator (or The Hero)

This is commonly the eldest child. This child is on the surface the most psychologically healthy, but actually they may be the poorest at asking for their own needs to be met or setting boundaries. This child as an adult may be prone to secret acts of rebellion – this could include disordered eating, private addiction issues or other compulsive behaviours. They often find themselves in a triangle with the Scapegoat and the Baby (see below), or the Scapegoat and the parents. Even if they find life to be exhausting, but will never show it; privately they will feel ignored, publicly they will maintain a happy demeanour.

The family system, while outwardly celebratory of this child, may in fact view the child for what they provide rather than who they truly are. They are the one who will always do the favour, they will never act up at school and they will always attend the family party. Inside this child might struggle with feeling that nothing they do is ever quite good enough and they will torture themselves with feelings of '99 per cent is not 100 per cent' throughout their life. They are likely to be an achiever and prize relationships and stability, but they will struggle with enforcing their own true emotional needs and will rarely show emotional vulnerability, preferring logical discussion rather than unbridled emotion.

We see examples of the Mediator child in older siblings caretaking for younger ones, or giving the toy over to the demanding child, sitting 'nicely' when asked to do so and generally being 'helpful'. Now there are of course many positives from developing this style of behaviour – this child is likely to do well at school and be well liked in social situations. They are also likely to focus on maintaining relationships in their adult life and, as result, often embrace the responsibility of parenting and marriage, but the key learning for this child is recognising their own needs and how to voice them.

The Scapegoat

This is commonly the second born child, but not necessarily. The most toxic example of triangulation is known as scapegoating. This is the one member who is a very convenient bucket for everybody's anxiety. This person is accused of being the troublemaker or the black sheep. I often see them accused of being 'mentally unstable', and in fact they are usually the one in family therapy that the family has come to get therapy about. This child has been blamed for every wrong in the family and is commonly thought of as a problem. They are likely to be the one that confronts the narcissistic parent's behaviour, and may on occasion stick up for their siblings. They may face crueller treatment and punishment than other children, and as a result they often carry the belief that they are unloved or unlovable.

The idea of the Scapegoat conjures up ideas of a rebellious character who has maybe addiction issues, antisocial issues, but the scapegoated child may be none of these things: they may be in fact a people pleaser, or a high achiever, particularly if that achievement has awarded them a higher status than their narcissistic parent and they are now the focus of jealousy. The Scapegoat might also be the child who is always called upon to caretake the parent or to nurse them in some way. The key thing here is the Scapegoat child is not seen as an individual, they are seen by the parent only for what they can provide for them. This may sound strange when we consider the child who is told they are the 'problem', but the narcissist sees the 'thing' that the child provides them is the fact they can be called the problem; now they can be used as being a receptacle for all the narcissist's anxiety, rage and shame. A common use of the 'problem' is a scapegoated child's mental health needs: this can be used by the family as a tool to direct any attention away from their dysfunction and on to the Scapegoat's 'mental health issues'.

Coping with being the Scapegoat in your family is far from easy and it is often not until adulthood that people realise that this has been done to them. I will share with you that the Scapegoat is often the family member with the highest amount of emotional bravery, resilience and honesty, as they are often the truth speaker. No family likes anyone to shine a light on their dysfunction, so recognising that you did that and you suffered for it is a painful process, but I'll leave you with this: most therapists I know were the Scapegoat of their family, including me ☺. To understand what it is to be scapegoated often means that you develop empathy for those who were also scapegoated.

I think the fact a lot of therapists tend to play this role in their family also suggests that those who do find themselves here often develop an interest in healing others and particularly in becoming trauma informed.

The Lost Child

Not every family has one of these but they are often the child born after the Mediator / Hero and the Scapegoat, and as a result of the Mediator trying their best to protect the Scapegoat from the narcissistic parent, the Mediator may not have a lot of sibling space left for this child. This is a child who the system often ignores – they are 'OK'. They might be loners, and are frequently avoidant in attachment patterns. On the surface they don't need much, and they find the family 'drama' exhausting; they appear to be very self-reliant.

I often see a great number of high-achieving adults who were the Lost Child; they work well alone, they don't require a lot of direction and they are generally considered self-sustaining. However, these adults are often told that they can be distant or unemotional in relationships, so in order to manage this role within their life, they need to learn to accept emotions rather than avoid them.

The Baby (or The Mascot)

Commonly thought of as the 'spoilt', what do we actually mean by this? I would suggest this character actually holds a huge amount of parental anxiety; you will commonly find the other siblings saying that this one 'got away with everything'. Let's think about that for a minute: why did they? Is it because this was the parent's last 'go' at parenting and they didn't want to risk yet another possible fractured relationship so they desperately tried to placate this child? Or was this the child who absorbed the apathy of their parents' struggling marriage – by the time they were born, divides had been drawn and the parents were not as aligned as they had been, so they parented separately rather than together as they had with previous children.

Family systems theory often refers to this child, common in fourth-born last-born children, as The Mascot – because their primary role in the system is to be a distraction; they are the clown and the entertainer. They distract the system from all of the anxieties that came before them and they often find themselves on the receiving end of all of the system's dysfunctions. This is a child who grew when the family system was exhausted of all of its resources and energy, and as a result we may see addiction being a more common occurrence in this child, as well as poor adult mental health.

This child is sometimes seen by the other siblings as the 'golden child', but what the child feels is actually a deep desire to escape the cloying focus of their parents, and they attempt to branch out on their own. Sometimes this is successful and the golden child continues to be hailed as a successful product of the family system, when actually they themselves feel smothered by it. More often than not, however, this child is not allowed to develop as an independent adult and finds themselves setting expectations they cannot live up to. They become very harsh critics of themselves and consequently often find themselves feeling a 'failure' or not living up to plans. They wanted desperately to be seen as a successful adult but they are babied and infantilised by the family system and they are not set up for success; the family system needs a figure which they can all direct their attention to.

This child is often well liked, they are light-hearted, friendly and charismatic, but they need to learn to take themselves seriously in order to encourage others to do the same.

'I DON'T HAVE FAVOURITES'

So now we know that children are given a role within the family as a result of complicated team dynamic, what does this actually do to the child? Let me start by telling you one of the most surprisingly honest things anyone has ever said to me, and it happened, rather unceremoniously, in the carpark of Melbourne airport. I was handing back a rental car to a jolly looking man, who smiled appreciatively at my first daughter.

'You just got one?' he asked.

'Yes,' I said.

'I got five,' he smiled.

'Oh, how wonderful.'

'You know what though . . . you always love your first the most. No one says it, but you do. You always love your first the most.'

I stood there open mouthed, as he handed me the rental agreement to sign. 'Have a great flight,' he said and, with that bombshell, off he went.

I have thought about that conversation many times over the years, and I agonised over whether that was true? Did I love my first daughter more than my second? Did my mother love my sister more than me? Never did that conversation come back to plague me more than when I was pregnant with my second child. Would that be reality, would I not love this child as much?

Pregnancy is a tough time for a lot of reasons, but your first pregnancy offers you an opportunity to imagine yourself as 'mother'. It opens the door to a new world and a new ideal – you can think of all the things you will do or not do, you can spend time reading parenting books and imagining how you will do things differently from the way your mother did.

By the time the second or third or fourth pregnancy rolls around, you likely have a view of yourself as 'mother' – for many women, they have endured the humbling years of early motherhood where they realise a lot of things they imagined didn't come to pass. They DID give screen time as a reward, and occasionally they resorted to bribery with sugar, hell they even shouted a few times – nothing was perfect, nothing was clean or contained, but in its own way, everything was OK. You formed a bond with this wonderful little being and you had your own little magical relationship. How on earth were you going to accommodate another one?

Previous pregnancy or childbirth experiences can also impact this time; previous trauma can deeply impact how you feel doing it all over again, as can previous experiences of post-natal depression.

If you suffered from a traumatic birth or a traumatic pregnancy, consider talking with a mental health professional BEFORE the baby arrives. Trauma within birth or pregnancy can be stored in a variety of different ways in the body: anxiety around your health / baby's health, feeling detached, feeling resentful, becoming irritated with people asking about the baby, replaying your previous experience in your head or imagining a negative outcome for this time. Birth Trauma Association offers wonderful advice and guidance for mothers who have had previously traumatic experiences either in labour or in postpartum care. Untreated birth trauma can cause postpartum depression and even later life anxiety: it is important that it is treated. Evidence-based treatments for birth trauma include EMDR and Trauma Focused CBT. Birth partners may also suffer birth trauma, and it is as imperative that they also seek help for this.

If you suffered postpartum depression the first time around, you are at a higher risk of experiencing it with future pregnancies. PPD is a well-researched and treatable condition that you do not need to suffer. If you previously felt low mood or anxiety following a birth, reach out to your health care provider to discuss possible options to manage any emerging symptoms. Speak to your partner and friends about your fears and discuss a care plan for this postpartum period.

HOW DO YOU EXPLAIN ANOTHER CHILD TO YOUR CHILD / CHILDREN?

The introduction of a new family member may not be greeted by your other offspring with the same excitement with which you view it. The addition of a new brother or sister, even for children who already have siblings, brings with it the news of 'change' and something being disrupted in their environment. They will possibly share some of your excitement, but also may feel jealousy and even some fear around being 'forgotten' or 'less loved', or having to share Mummy / Daddy. This is reasonable and normal – infinity is a difficult concept for adults to grasp so to tell a child, 'I can love more than one child unconditionally,' may feel false or confusing to them. I often use an analogy about space: I ask them, can you see the beginnings and end of space? Why is that? I then offer the analogy that love is like space – it goes on and on and never gets bigger or smaller, there are over a billion stars in our galaxy alone, and they all get the same amount of space to grow in. Some grow bigger and some grow smaller, but the space that surrounds them stays the same. It is never ending. Love is like that.

For some children, however, the thought of sharing Mummy, and even the idea of sharing their sibling with another child, may feel traumatic. They might feel like they are losing their family model, and life as they know it is about to change irrevocably – no matter what they do. Allow them their own space to exist in and to think and feel. Remember that being a child is constantly living in a changing world that you didn't ask for and can't control. This can be a frightening experience and they may need some extra support to help process this turbulence of transition.

Extract–Express–Reflect for the new sibling

Extract

Invite your child to ask any questions they might have about this new baby and try to be as honest as possible in your answers.

Express

Encourage your child to give their feelings a name, and remind them that it's OK to not have 'all happy' feelings about this. If they have fears, or anger or jealousy, you are ready and willing to talk about this with them. Make it clear, however, that a child is not a reversible decision, so while they are welcome to feel something about it, they cannot change it. But you are here to help them process this change. Your mantra here is: 'All feelings are welcome.'

Reflect

Try to invite your child where possible to feel included in the planning for the baby; encourage them to see the baby as their family and describe the baby as 'our baby'. The child can find a sense of belonging with the baby if the baby is discussed as part of 'their' family. Discuss the role they will have in the baby's care – if they would like it, and what it means to be a brother / sister. Explore any thoughts or fears they might have in relation to this.

WHAT IS SIBLING RIVALRY?

Research suggests that sibling conflict occurs on average eight times an hour, and that sisters tend to be the closest, but sibling relationships that include a brother tend to develop the most aggression: early and middle years of childhood tend to see a spike in aggression with most tailing off somewhere towards adolescence. Sibling rivalry actually has a developmental cause – it helps children to assert themselves as unique and special and ultimately worthy of attention. Psychologists call this process 'differentiation' and believe it helps children to develop their own personalities, assert individual differences and understand how to establish boundaries around wants and needs. However, as any parent will tell you, this process of 'differentiation' doesn't always appear developmentally useful, or healthy – it can be one of the hardest challenges a parent faces.

Sibling rivalry is the squabbling and jealousy that can occur between siblings and usually happens as a result of:

- A need for attention from a parent
- A desire to get attention from one or all of their siblings
- A desire to maintain or gain power over the family dynamic

Let's look at these areas individually, beginning with the most common reasons for sibling rivalry: competing for the attention of a parent.

Why do children feel the need to compete for parental attention?

From babyhood, children recognise the adults in their life as necessary sources of survival – the adults provide food, warmth, shelter and love. The consideration of sharing this with another being feels alarming and scary; after all, very few of us would jump at the chance to halve our source of survival.

Now consider this for a moment: a first child knows what it is to have 100 per cent of a parent's attention without any competing child, a second child ONLY knows a life where a parent's attention is halved or shared. Third and fourth children equally only know a life where this attention is divided even more. It is understandable then how subsequent children may grow up to understand that everything is a competition, and that first children may feel that everything is worth 'protecting'.

These suggestions also assume that the first child gets 100 per cent of a parent's attention 100 per cent of the time, which is highly unlikely. The parent has their own outside focuses

— a relationship / marriage, work commitments, other family members, social commitments. The child may feel that the parent's world is a place of competing forces and that their time is a commodity to fight over.

Signs of rivalry for attention

- Deliberately 'starting' arguments with a sibling in order to gain a reaction from a parent. Remembering that any attention can be considered attention, particularly to young children, and if your child often finds themselves in the midst of arguments that result in you or the other parent sitting down and talking to them / shouting at them / trying to negotiate or reason with them, consider if this may not be the result of poor conflict resolution within your child; they may actually be demanding your attention.

- Playing the victim or finding narratives that blame or shame the other sibling. Sympathy garnering is another prime indicator of competing for attention; sympathy can often feel nice to a child – it might involve special treatment, cuddles or dedicated focus.

- Accusing you of 'loving him / her more than me' – this is a child's way of expressing their jealousy and inner shame by projecting this bad feeling on to you. By accusing you of being unloving or unequal in your love they find an outlet for these upsetting and distressing anxieties that maybe your love is limited and there is not enough to go round.

What do you do about it?

- Make individual time for each child. This can feel like a very difficult thing to manage when you have multiple children in the home so might mean dividing time between parents and each spending dedicated time with each child, or on a rotating basis.
- Create 'special one-on-one time' with your child. This can be for a few hours, a day, or a whole weekend. During this time the child, rather than the adult, is responsible for setting the activities / agenda. Consequently they have the novel and empowering experience of being completely in control and being gratified (within reasonable practical and financial limits of course!). Ideally, love-bombing sessions should be between one parent and one child. During the activities the parent, through words and behaviour, constantly illustrates how much they unconditionally love their child. This demonstrates to the child that their own behaviour (past, present and future) has no bearing on the parent's love or commitment to them.
- Celebrate your children as individuals and never, ever compare. Negative comparison is the foundation of jealousy – negative comparison creates a narrative that a child tells themselves they are lesser than another, or they have not in some way made the grade.
- Remember this phrase: 'Every petal is beautiful, but no petal is the same.' I tell my girls every day that the opposite of jealousy is self-assurance – jealousy tells us that we are not enough and we must take from others or hurt others in order to exist, but when we

celebrate our own uniqueness, we remember that we are complete, perfect and enough ... just as we are. Everything unique has no competition because it has no comparison.

- Remind your child every day that they are enough, just by being themselves – without even trying, they are special and loved.

- Model asking for attention in a healthy way, so get your child to practise saying, 'Can I please have some time with you Mum / Dad?', and respond as much as possible, immediately. If for whatever reason you are not able to give immediate attention, acknowledge your child and make a plan together for when you can spend time together. 'Thank you so much for asking me and I really would love to do that, can I just finish this – it will take me five minutes and then let's do that.' It is very important that when you are teaching children to ask for attention in a positive way that they receive a positive response. If they ask in a healthy way and don't receive attention, they are less likely to continue with this method and will likely resort to, or return to, less healthy methods.

- Reinforce positive play! This looks like:
  1. Be interested in what your children are playing and asking to join in (when they are playing well together!).
  2. Complimenting their 'play relationship' together by saying things like, 'You look like you are having fun.'
  3. Compliment younger children in particular for taking turns.

4. Take a photo of them playing together nicely and put it in their play space.

Sibling rivalry for sibling attention

A less discussed form of sibling disruption / rivalry is actually a demand for a sibling's attention rather than a parent's. It is particularly common for a younger sibling, or a less socially mature sibling (such as a neurodiverse sibling) to demand attention from their brother / sister in a way that annoys them.

What does this look like?
- Hitting, scratching, biting a sibling
- Breaking toys or hiding them
- Deliberately annoying or irritating the sibling
- Ignoring the rules of a game and 'creating' an argument
- Playing a victim or blaming a sibling for upsetting them / leaving them out / not playing with them

What can you do about it?
- Encourage friendships and outlets outside of the sibling relationship so that the sibling relationship is not the only social exposure the younger sibling or the neurodiverse sibling has.
- Create an environment where the play space can be inclusive and easily shared; for example, place toys around that require two or more players. Try to include toys or a stimulus that all siblings can partake in, or at least all siblings can learn to partake in.
- Where possible offer a space for each sibling to have their own time and area, encourage each of them to

respect space and privacy and explain that they need to be invited into spaces that are individual.

- Model good 'play language' – show siblings how to ask to join games, and to ask to be shown rules. Ask older siblings for ideas around how to include their younger sibling or their neurodiverse sibling.

- Having a set time of day where there are no screens and imaginative play is encouraged can be a wonderful container for encouraging play time together. This structure helps younger siblings feel they will get their turn, and also teaches older siblings that it is important to dedicate time to their sibling relationship.

Sibling rivalry for power

Sometimes siblings fight in order to exert power over the other; this is often found within families whereby one of the adults uses this technique in order to exert or maintain power over the family dynamic as a whole. Sometimes this can simply be a developmental phase and children are experimenting with how much power they have and where their social boundaries are – this is normal. However, if this desire for power over another is left unchecked it can become bullying or intimidation, which is clearly unhealthy behaviour.

Children will look for power in a number of ways, and from a young age they realise that adults have a lot more power than they do. In houses where discipline is unpredictable or overly punitive this power craving can become overwhelming for children. They may start to believe that in order to survive, they need to dominate or control another, as they feel their world is overly controlled. A child who is trying to feel powerful over a weaker or younger child, and is doing it in order to intimidate or dominate, is showing that they feel weak or shamed in other areas of their life, and it requires an adult to explore with them in a compassionate manner why that might be.

What does this look like?

- Deliberately getting a sibling into trouble, such as encouraging a sibling to do something 'naughty' and then watching the consequences.
- Deliberately removing or hiding a toy of a younger sibling in order to cause confusion or distress.
- Bullying type behaviour such as ridiculing or belittling a sibling.
- Physically dominating a smaller or weaker sibling.
- Games whereby the younger or weaker sibling has to be subservient to the older or stronger sibling, or is only allowed to play if certain rules are followed.
- Games whereby a sibling is ridiculed, frightened or harmed for 'fun'.

What can you do about it?

- Avoid blaming if you did not see what happened. This is easier said than done, but where possible invite each sibling to tell their version of events and agree a narrative among you. It can be easy to jump to conclusions and we have all been guilty of snap discipline when we are at the end of our tether, but in order to show a fair power balance, it is imperative that all children feel they have equal say and an equal share of your attention.
- When you come into a room of upset or conflict, instead of resorting to disciplinary action, ask everyone, 'What

do we need to happen so that everyone can have a nice time?'

- Call out bullying behaviour (however subtle) straight away by:

   1. Acknowledging: 'I notice you keep getting your brother to do that'

   2. Enquiring: 'I wonder how he feels about that?' and

   3. Empathising: 'how would you feel about doing that?'

- Imprint the message firmly among all members of the house: anger is welcome here but aggression is not. Aggressive behaviour such as name calling, hitting, pushing or biting has no place in family relationships. Siblings can be angry with each other and they will become aggressive with each other, but it is so important that you enforce a message: you can be angry with your brother / sister, but I won't let you hurt them.

HOW YOU CAN MODEL HEALTHY SIBLING DYNAMICS IN YOUR HOME

The reality is all siblings fight, and while we would all like to see our little darlings playing nicely with each other at all times, they won't. Conflict and boundary pushing are a normal part of growing up, but it is our job as parents to help our children navigate this stage of life in as healthy a way as possible. So, what can we do to make our homes healthy?

- Allow your children their OWN relationship. Above all things, attempt to remove yourself as the 'tent peg' to

181

their relationship. Allow them space, privacy and time to play together without your involvement and without your interruption / refereeing. Encourage a message that their relationship is special and they are each other's family as much as they are YOUR family. A sibling relationship is likely to be much longer than that of parent / child, and when you are gone their relationship will be the lasting legacy of the home you created; help it to be as compassionate as possible.

- Face your own fear of loving one child more than the other. This is a normal and natural anxiety when you introduce another child to your family; acknowledge it and reflect upon it. It can be important to speak to a mental health professional if you have fears of not having 'enough love to go around' as it is likely a reflection not on your capacity as a parent, but on your experience of being parented.

- Face your own 'narcissism' as a parent. Parenting tells us that we need to be all things to our child, and for some parents having a child who always 'wants Mummy' can serve to fill a space or emptiness inside us where we feel inadequate or unloved in some way. This is not healthy and not helpful for your child – your role as a parent is to tell your child THEY can be their whole world, they do not need to look to you for approval; they have your approval inherently.

- Own your own 'power craving'; acknowledge and recognise any spaces within your parenting journey where you have tried to use power to make up for times you have felt out of control as a parent or when you have felt powerless. We are given a huge amount of power as adults, and we often use this power in ways that serve to cover up our own insecurities when faced with parenting choices or situations that we don't know how to navigate.

- Love is abundant. There is no limit on love and there is enough to fill every child and every adult within your family. When we remind children and ourselves that there is always enough love, we reduce the need for competition and the fear of lack or scarcity within ourselves.

The above may be read by some parents, myself included, with a head-in-the-hands type feeling of 'I wish I had . . .' or, 'I know I haven't . . .' Remember attachment is a lifelong process. Just because there may have been times in your life where you have prioritised one child's needs over another does not mean it's all set in stone now and nothing can be repaired. If you have read this chapter and recognised that one child has been taking more attention than another, or one child is acting out for your attention, be kind to yourself and acknowledge there were probably very real reasons for this dynamic. Maybe one child had more immediate needs, or maybe during the baby stages of another child you were going through your own changes in work or your environment – this is OK! Life happens, and it's all OK! Re-read the tips above and think about how you can incorporate them into your life NOW and how you can use these tips to re-set the attention in the house.

It can feel overwhelming and exhausting to care for multiple children, but remembering the rule of the magic 20 minutes (see page 76), when you break it down children actually require less one-on-one time than you might think. Try to take some time with each of your children individually and find out what is going on in their world currently – who they are playing with, what they are into. Take 20 minutes to have a chat with each of them or play with them. On occasions, take time to go and spend longer periods of time with each of them to create quality in-depth attachment memories together.

And never forget: attachment is a process, nothing is ever broken.

CHAPTER 10: DIVORCE / FAMILY SEPARATION

While I use the word divorce throughout this chapter, I am referring to the separation of any relationship where children are present. Divorce is deeply traumatic for the whole family and there will be a significant amount of grief felt during this process. For that reason, I would strongly advise both parents to seek mental support, be that a professional or friends and family. A divorce is a bereavement, a death of a life together, a life hoped for, and dreams made – and the emotional impact can take people by surprise. If you yourself have not experienced a divorce I would still recommend reading this chapter to gain greater understanding of what might be happening at home for those you know who have.

One of the subjects I get asked about more than any other in relation to family trauma is how we explain divorce to children. An often-quoted statistic is that one in two marriages ends in divorce; when I hear this, I wonder how much we consider the reality of that message. That's a lot of adults going through a significant life-altering trauma, and a lot of children experiencing major attachment rupture. People glaze over divorce as a commonplace event, without actually considering that this is the separation of a home, the separation of a family unit, and the death of a couple's vision for the future. No couple plans their wedding day imagining that one day they will be exchanging angry letters via lawyers over school holiday arrangements, the car payments and the kitchen cabinets.

When something happens to a lot of people, we assume it's 'not that bad' – but the reality is that divorce is one of the most painful things a person can go through, and many couples would cite the adversarial jousting by lawyers as one of the worst parts of the process. I think a lot of couples go into the process thinking, 'we will keep this pleasant, we will just split everything half and half', then they find during the legal process they become much more greedy or resentful. Divorce is a legal process, a lawyer's job is to get the best deal for their client, and they can be ruthless in that pursuit. However, this can mean they lose sight of the fact that to the client, the 'other side' is not simply an opponent; it used to be their spouse.

HOW TO HANDLE TRAUMA FOLLOWING DIVORCE

Divorce is life-altering and many people will view their life as a pre-divorce phase and a post-divorce phase. Many people, however, find that they grow positively following a divorce, but this post-trauma growth is exhausting. It might take months, or even years, of soul searching and resilience building to get to this healing stage. Nobody imagines themselves pitted against the person they once fell in love with, and no one imagines feeling hatred for someone they once considered their life partner. For many people recovering from divorce, it is this adjustment in their world view that feels the most traumatic – to consider that the person they once loved most in the world would now be someone they feel estranged from, or simply feel nothing for, is incredibly distressing and even debilitating.

The pain will eventually pass and the way you feel now will not remain forever, but there are things you can do to help yourself:

- **Accept your emotions:** It is normal to experience difficult, distressing emotions following a divorce. Work on accepting what you feel without trying to deny or judge yourself.
- **Seek professional help when needed:** If you are feeling paranoid, or intensely anxious, or you have started to engage in risk-taking behaviour, it is time to get help from a professional. If you have suicidal thoughts, it is imperative that you seek psychological help that may include a combination of medication and therapy, as directed by a medical professional.

- **Seek social support:** Having the support of friends and family is essential. Sharing your feelings with others can relieve distress and help you feel less alone. This may be particularly hard if your friends are mutual friends with your ex-partner – focus on spending time with people who do not trigger your anxiety or low mood, and be very selective to only focus on those who help to increase your confidence and overall happiness. This does not mean you have to avoid mutual friends forever, but in the immediate aftermath of the trauma it is important to surround yourself with people who serve your highest good. This is not the time to be altruistic, or the bigger person – you need to be self-serving in order to heal.
- **Take time to heal:** Give yourself a break and focus on caring for yourself emotionally and physically. If this means taking time off work, or cutting down on your social schedule, so be it; in the same way you would take time to heal after a car crash, take time to mentally heal after a trauma.

REMEMBER THE PERSON YOU ALWAYS WERE

It is likely that somewhere during the course of your marriage or relationship you 'merged' with the other person; that is not to say that you lost something or that you changed something consciously, but within many long-term marriages people start to merge together in order to form a unit. A much beloved teacher of mine once told me a rather bemusing analogy about 'the life of a couple': we all start out, according to him, as happy potatoes growing in the ground. We then wonder if we would like to become boiled potatoes. Happy and solid and boiling away in a pan with another potato, eventually we decide that we would like to join and merge and become mashed potatoes. Then we realise that life as mash is hard – we are softer, weaker and less noticed as individual potatoes, so we go back to being boiled potatoes.

While I always thought the comparison of people to potatoes was a little odd, I got the analogy. We spend large amounts of our life wishing to be, trying to be, or living as if we are a conjoined entity. But in the end we find this shared identity tiring and we crave our own individuality again. Many healthy long-term relationships manage to go through this process of differentiation and maintain the connection of love and mutual respect. However, some relationships find this overwhelming, and they simply cannot live through the differences to find a desire to remain with this person as two loving individuals – they need to separate.

Following this decision to separate, many people often find themselves returning to the things they liked, the dreams they had, the person they were or wanted to be prior to the relationship. This can be a wonderfully fulfilling process – I have witnessed many of my clients go through a divorce and emerge the other side with a revised and renewed identity. I have seen people return to education, develop new hobbies, lose / gain weight, move countries and, of course, meet new people.

WHAT ARE WE GOING TO TELL THE KIDS?

We have already discussed that it is important to start making plans and space for your life post-divorce. What new freedom or hope might this change bring you? How do you think you will see yourself in 10 years' time? A divorce can feel overwhelming, but this too will pass, and with a lot of maturity and diplomacy you can move to a space where the family that once was inhabits spaces together fairly harmoniously. Do not, however, underestimate the impact on your children; while you have been married maybe half of your life, they may have been in this family their entire life. This is literally their whole world and it's being ruptured; they have no idea who they are outside of this model as they have never existed without it.

Be compassionate and acknowledge that they too will go through a period of grief, and that may involve anger towards you.

Children often look for a container for their difficult feelings, particularly those of anger or loss. Unfortunately, in the case of divorce this often means that they will direct those feelings towards one parent in particular. In the world of children there is always a goodie and a baddie. Ambivalence is an adult concept that they cannot yet grasp – remember that children's brains do not learn the entire concept of empathy until they are 25 so it is very likely that they will not understand the idea of a 'conscious uncoupling' and that they will look to create a narrative whereby one party is the cause or the instigator. Don't be alarmed by this, and don't attempt to enforce the adult idea of 'everybody has a part to play in this' too early; for a child below the age of 13 it is highly unlikely they will grasp this concept. Even for a teenager, they may understand in a small part that no one was at 'fault', but to ask them to consider adult concepts of dissonance between couples, or dynamics of marriage, is way beyond their grasp.

Extract–Express–Reflect for divorce or separation

Extract

Setting and space will be very key to having this discussion – try to allow the child to dictate a space they feel is safe. This may not for example be in the marital home, or it may be in your ex-partner's home. Let them choose – processing divorce is one the biggest ruptures a child will face to their immediate world. Allow them the control around where they will have this talk with you. Also, in this circumstance more than any other, allow them the timing. Normally when we use this tool as a 'debriefing' exercise we are focusing on a singular traumatic event and looking for ways that the child can regain agency. In the example of divorce, we will stick to our three main parts of Extract–Express–Reflect but we have to acknowledge that some of their most difficult feelings of anger or sadness may be directed towards you. So for this reason do not pressure your child to talk to you in the 48-hour window after something has happened – allow them the control to answer yes to the question, 'Please may I talk to you?'

Assuming you have found a suitable time and space to have this talk, get into the fact-finding stage. Ask them simple questions such as what would they like to know? Children have very little understanding of adult relationships – they will not grasp the idea of marriage, let alone divorce. They may surprise you by being focused on practicalities such as, 'Which house will I live in?' or, 'What will happen with the dog?' Their world is one of 'known things' that provide safety, and 'unknown things' are scary. They will require a lot of reassurance about who will do what and when.

They will need simple and firm explanations. Do not overwhelm them with emotional detail or information they cannot process. Stick to the basics such as: which parent will be moving out, where the child will live, who will look after them and how often they will see the other parent. Be prepared for questions; provide short answers, then wait to see if there are more.

Express

Children may look for an explanatory narrative for the split, and they may assign blame or cause to events or one parent. They may also imagine ways they can 'get Mummy and Daddy back together'. It is important to acknowledge that children often look for metaphorical containers to process big feelings – they may apply ideas that they have seen in books, TV programmes or games to their real life. This is part of their grieving process. So all these ideas around ways they can 'get Mummy and Daddy back together' are part of their processing – they need to work through this to see that this situation is final. Don't stop them sharing these ideas, allow them to come out as part of their grief.

Ask them about their feelings in relation to the change, questions such as, 'What is the thing you are most worried about?', or reminding them that 'it's OK to be mad at Mummy and Daddy'. Do not assign blame, and do not try to minimise their feelings – allow the space to be about them and what they feel about this.

Remember at all times that while you are grieving the loss of your marriage, which may be something that has felt like forever for you, for your child the parental relationship really has been forever. Keep your thoughts about your ex-partner to yourself; your job is to protect their idea of their parent rather than to defend your position. While your ex was ONCE your spouse, they will ALWAYS be their parent; treat that with the respect it deserves.

Reflect

Allow them the space to work through these big feelings, and this conversation will likely take multiple discussions, all of which may go off on many different tangents before it gets to the reflect stage. In fact, you might find yourself stuck in the express stage for much longer than you hoped. That goes for both you and your child!

Once the feelings about the split have been vocalised and acknowledged, try to craft a narrative where there is no 'baddie', the divorce was not over one thing – it was a decision to no longer live together anymore as you felt unhappy with each other. It was not, however, a decision to stop loving them, and they were in no way the cause of the split. It is important that this is always enforced, as children will often believe that their 'behaviour' is the biggest threat to harmony in the house – if I am bad, bad things will happen. So they may feel that deep down they caused this.

Over time, start to work towards a space where you can identify the positives that have happened as a result of the decision to split. Your child may always feel that the divorce will be viewed as a bereavement and they cannot find anything positive in this – that's OK. If this is where they are, do not push a narrative of 'I am happier now', even if you are. The focus here is on them, not you. You can re-enforce the idea of how resilient they have been, and how much you love them.

INTRODUCING A NEW PARTNER
TO YOUR CHILD

Deciding to introduce a new partner to your child can be a major milestone post-divorce. The key factor to a successful introduction is time: do not introduce a partner to your children whom you have not given yourself the time to accept as your partner, and do not introduce a new partner to your child when they haven't yet had the time to accept that Mummy and Daddy no longer live together.

It is highly possible that your child will not accept your new partner; this is OK. Just because you have chosen them as a partner, it does not mean that they have to. They may consider the person the cause of the breakup of their family, particularly if they suspect an affair – it is then understandable that they will not welcome this person into their life, and they might feel that by being nice to this person they are in some way betraying their other parent. Discuss these feelings with them and give them space and time to be open and honest with you.

It can be tempting in the first throes of a relationship, particularly post a messy divorce, to lose yourself within that relationship and to want other people to be 'happy for you', but it can be too big a leap to expect your child to be one of these people. They may find the concept of a new person a sobering and saddening thought – this person represents the death of their parents' marriage. Help your child to move through this phase, by allowing them the choice of whether or not they choose to meet your new partner. If they consent to meeting them, allow them also to choose the location and the length of the meeting.

Be open to your child's request to change the plan at the last minute or to leave early; at all times remember the child may be battling intensely conflicting feelings about this meeting and it may be overwhelming for them. Keep that message in mind: a child's emotional centre is not yet fully developed until the age of 25, and just because you can process transition, does not mean they can.

During the meeting, keep the physical contact between you and your new partner to a minimum, and keep the meeting light and easy. Do not introduce the person as their new step-parent or a replacement of the other parent, and make it clear that your child does not have to have a relationship with them until they are ready.

Even if you have had a successful introduction of a new partner, ensure your child has enough time to spend with you alone. Do not bring your new partner to every outing, and wait until your child is ready to consider a shared living arrangement. The key to a happy blended family is: time, low pressure and compassion.

So what about if YOU need to meet your new partner's children, or if you become a step-parent?

HOW TO NAVIGATE BECOMING A STEP-PARENT

Why is step-parenthood sometimes seen as challenging? Well, firstly, the fairytales that include a wicked stepmother definitely don't help the image, and nor does the fact that step-parenthood often follows a period of trauma, be that divorce or death, so in many ways a step-parent is off to a difficult start. It is not easy parenting from a place where you have already formed a biological attachment to a child, let alone parenting from a place where you have entered the child's life at school age or adolescence. It is also a very tricky line to tread of being a 'guardian' but NOT a parent. As a step-parent you may face constant reminders that you are not the biological parent and that you have a very specific set of boundaries to manage. This can be draining and emotionally turbulent, particularly if you would like to play more of a 'parent' role with your step-child but you are facing pushback in doing so from certain people.

As a step-parent you are unwittingly thrown into the middle of this emotional turbulence simply by virtue of having a relationship with one of the child's parents. For some children this can mean that they direct their pain and confusion towards you – in essence, you become the enemy, or even the reason for the breakdown of their original family. It's hard not to feel indignation at this, and it's hard to not get angry about being on the receiving end of this blame and guilt, but you have to remind yourself that this child has, in their eyes, lost a parent.

A step-parent may also be thrown into a world of domesticity and child rearing that they previously had no knowledge of. If this is your first experience of caring for a child you may find that all of a sudden you are dealing with homework, discipline, school runs and meal times. You might find this new world challenging, tiring or even boring. You also might find that your relationship with your partner feels dominated by their role as parent and you in turn have to conform to this family unit in ways you don't want to or are not used to. A step-parent essentially enters a family without any preparation and it can all feel like a bomb explosion.

- Tip one: remember this child has a lot more to adapt to than you. They have lost their previous family model. Show compassion and understanding, even if occasionally it is through gritted teeth.

- Tip two: don't try to do too much too soon; allow relationships and attachment to develop naturally. Don't force it – let the child come to you.
- Tip three: be yourself, because everybody else is taken! Nobody expects or needs you to be the carbon copy of the biological parent. Let your step-child see you as an individual and allow your relationship to form uniquely and organically.

Relationships are built over time

Develop or suggest activities you can do together; don't expect them to rush at once and don't even expect gratitude in the first instance. But keep offering suggestions and ideas, and wait for them to take you up on it. Communication is key – let them into your life and let them get to know you. Be warm and inviting, but not pushy in your affection. Allow the child their space and take their lead.

Never bad-mouth the other parent

It should go without saying that as a step-parent you should never bad-mouth the biological parent. Even if the child does, simply listen and validate their feelings, but never engage in bitching or gossip. Know your limits when it comes to disciplining the child and enforcing rules – perhaps discuss this with your partner in the first instance and understand that you may have to bite your tongue if your views are not in agreement with those of the biological parent.

BLENDED FAMILY Q&A

My partner has children from a previous relationship, and I feel nervous about meeting them for the first time – do you have any advice?

Discuss your concerns with your partner and agree a way that you can be introduced to the child. Decide on terms you might use to describe your relationship. Maybe even role-play some answers to questions. When you do meet the child, with all of this in mind, be led by them as to how much information you share or how much interaction you have with them on that first meeting. Be warm, be friendly, be interested, but don't be pushy.

I've just become a step-parent and I'd like to introduce them to my own older children. How should I navigate this?

Discuss in the first instance with your children how they feel about meeting your step-children; maybe they have an idea where they would like to meet them and how. Your first responsibility should be to your biological children and ensuring that they feel comfortable and secure with the details of the meeting, then take it from there. Ensure your partner does the same with their children so that each set of siblings feels protected, listened to and validated.

My young step-children are shy and haven't warmed to me yet. How can I nurture the relationship?

Take your time. They have lost a family model. While you may not feel they have gone through a trauma, or maybe you feel that the previous family model was not good for the children, they have gone through an extreme period of emotional turbulence. Be engaging, ask questions and make suggestions. Allow them to take the lead and let them guide you as to how and when they form a relationship with you.

I'm not sure what my role is as a step-mother within our blended family. How can I carve out a position for myself?

It's not down to you to carve out a position; your position is already defined by nature of your relationship. If you would like to develop a relationship that is individual between you and your step-children, this must come from them. With even the best of intentions and the kindest of gestures, attempting to force a relationship with step-children rarely ends in anything but disaster. Sit back, be patient, be yourself and allow them to come to you. Let them see you are a nonthreatening, trustworthy presence and the rest will follow.

I'm about to have a baby and I'm nervous my step-children will feel jealous of the new arrival. How can I make them feel included?

Discuss with them how they feel about the baby, and ask them how they would like to refer to the baby. Involve them in the activities of caring for the baby (if they want to!). Try to set some time aside to engage with them in one-on-one time or special activities so that they feel included and not left out.

My step-son often says, 'You're not my real mum' during tantrums. How do I respond to this?

Well in the first instance, he is correct. Acknowledge this, as hard as it may seem. It is an accurate statement that you are not his biological mother and that hurts him. What he is trying to convey is that it hurts him that there is change in his life, and he is feeling overwhelmed and confused. Give him space to say this and feel those feelings. You can simply respond with, 'I know. But I care for you very much.' There is no point attempting to gloss over or distract the child from his very real feelings of pain and anger – it is better to offer a safe space for him to feel these emotions and let him know that you won't be scared off by them. You are safe, you are consistent, and you are there.

HOW TO TALK TO NEURODIVERSE CHILDREN ABOUT DIVORCE

- ADHD children are often impulsive and may be prone to behaviours that are attention seeking in their appearance in response to life-disrupting news such as divorce.
- They may also attempt to find a way to make it right, using all their creative thought processes but also combined with their difficulty to control impulse – this may result in them saying things that cause offence or hurt.
- ASC children will find any change in their living circumstance deeply upsetting and they might go through a period of meltdown or shutdown in response to this news.
- Give ASC children a lot of space to ask questions and to set their own parameters for their new living situation. This might mean helping them to decorate a bedroom in their new house or helping them to agree to who does what in relation to their care.
- Note that ASC children can become very controlling as a response to their anxiety around change; allow some control to a point, but be firm on boundaries where offering control would be inappropriate.

CHAPTER 11:
LOSS /
BEREAVEMENT

One of parenting's most challenging questions is, 'What does death mean?', even more so when we must tell a child that someone or something has died. Death is triggering to us in many ways. It forces us to face our own fears and questions about mortality, it reminds us of our experiences of loss, and it forces us to face the idea of a grieving process. Death can be represented in a number of ways; I have heard countless people tell me they don't like hospitals as it reminds them of death, or that they don't like to walk past graveyards / crematoriums as they 'think about dead people'. So what do we tell children when they ask us, 'Where do people go when they die?'

The first and most important part of conveying death to a child, no matter the age, is that death is a final physical state; this person (or pet) will no longer be here to see us. No matter what your own family's spiritual beliefs are, chances are they will concur with the idea that the body once dead is no longer walking around. We can help to explain this to a child by saying: 'The person won't be with us on earth anymore.'

It can be useful if the child asks questions about why the body is dead to say things like 'the heart stopped working, and they can't live without that' or 'they have stopped breathing'. Children do better with short, concrete explanations – it is not necessary to offer flowery metaphors; a simple the person 'can't live anymore as they aren't breathing' can suffice.

It is equally a bad idea to equate death with getting old – children do not have a concept of time or age, to them 40 is the same as 80, so when you say, 'Oh I am getting old,' a young child may equate this to being elderly and near death. Do not mix age and death. It also, sadly, can open you up to very difficult questions around the death of young people, if this tragedy is something you ever need to explain. There is of course no need to dwell on the cause of death, particularly in the case of death by violent causes or by accidents. This is overwhelming and deeply traumatic for children.

Be prepared for emotions – both theirs and yours. It is completely OK and can be helpful to show your own emotions surrounding death in front of children. Contrary to what you might think, it is not traumatic for children to see a parent grieving. It helps to teach them that emotions in response to death are normal. This can help prevent any numbing or dissociation that they may develop in relation to death or grief. The mantra is always: all emotions are welcome here.

It can be very helpful to introduce your own spiritual beliefs about the afterlife and death if this helps you to process death. So if you do believe in heaven, it's OK to share your beliefs with children. It can be very relieving for them to be asked what their beliefs are, as when we ask them to consider this we ask them to engage the emotional processing part of the brain. You might be amazed to listen to the response from even very young children, to the question, 'What do you think happens to people after they die?' Children often use metaphor to process big emotions or messages – let them use their imagination to process death if it helps them.

If you don't have particularly strong spiritual beliefs or this subject makes you uncomfortable you can simply say 'I don't know' to these questions, and it is also OK to show children that death remains one of the biggest mysteries of life. It is helpful to explain the cycle of life to children: 'All things die, and like plants / animals / and all life, so do humans. But dying doesn't mean forgetting.' We can encourage children to hold the idea that the person may no longer be physically here, but they can be here in our memory, and our memory of them is no less precious because it is finite: love is infinite.

CHILDREN'S REACTION TO DEATH BY DIFFERENT AGES

Toddlers and pre-school

- Children of this age will have very little concept of time, so things like permeance or infinity are too abstract for them.
- Stick to: 'I would love to see them again, but we can't once someone has died.'

- Children of this age may experience a very physical reaction to grief and this can appear as bed-wetting, a regression in toilet training or a change in eating habits or mood.

Primary school

- Children of this age can understand more complex concepts such as 'forever' but this does not mean they will fully grasp the idea of death.
- This is not an age to introduce any discussions about causes of death, it is better to stick to basic explanations such as 'stopped breathing' or 'heart stopped'.
- Nightmares or sleep disturbances are a common reaction to death at this stage of development, where the imagination is working overtime.
- We may also see the child start to project anxieties about health or death on to other things; this is a passing phase but if it develops into a behaviour that is disrupting their normal basic functioning, it might be helpful to speak to a professional.
- Children's imaginations are working very hard at this age and they can be prone to attributing cause to magical causes or to themselves. It is imperative that you remind the child there is nothing they did or could have done to prevent or cause this situation.

Aged 11–15

- Children of this age very likely have their own ideas about spirituality or afterlife. It can be helpful to discuss these with them.

- At this age, children can process basic facts around causes of death such as the name of an illness or very factual statements around the cause. Be careful not to overload them with elaborate descriptions or shocking information.
- It is not uncommon for children this age to not want to process the death or talk about it. This is OK; give them their space and let them know you are there for them whatever they need.

WHEN DO CHILDHOOD FEARS RELATED TO DEATH BECOME A 'PROBLEM'?

If you are the parent of a 'worrier' or a child who is prone to repetitive behaviour as a 'control response' to anxiety, managing grief responses may require you to manage this desire for 'control'. For these children a positive example is crucial, but even more so is encouraging the articulation of thoughts. In the mind of the 'worrier' child, fears that might have been internalised (such as beliefs around death, illness, loss) might have become so overwhelming that the thoughts are intrusive, and in order to reduce these thoughts you might see repetitive behaviour, such as obsessive questioning or rituals.

In an adult, we might describe this as OCD, and indeed in extreme cases this might be accurate in a child, but following news of a death a child might respond with more 'anxious control' behaviour than they would normally, which doesn't constitute OCD. It does however require some help from an adult to help neutralise the worry. The key to engaging with intrusive thought patterns and breaking the fear that creates them is three-fold:

1. **Name the emotion:** for pre-school children, this might require adult input to help differentiate emotional states such as fear vs frustration; for older children it may require the adult to offer their own experiences as a model: 'I feel like this, how about you?', 'I think if that were me I might feel . . .', 'I'm wondering if what you feel is . . .'

2. **Articulate the worry:** allowing someone to express their fear is one of the most relieving things we can do; it reduces the power of the worry and allows it to come out in the open. Remind your child that no fear is 'silly' or 'embarrassing' and that they are allowed to say anything to you if it is causing them distress.

3. **Ground the situation in fact:** no worry is irrational, there is some grain of truth in everything we might fear – anything can truly happen. What is key to managing this is acknowledging the probability of it occurring. Many fears and worries are not grounded in fact; for example it might be helpful to remind children of the facts around the death and how these facts do not apply to them. Then get them to consider how likely something is to happen as well as how likely it is to not happen.

Grief is a sad, confusing time for everyone, and children are no different. It's understandable that little minds might struggle to make sense of this concept, just as adults do. Remind children that it is OK to feel many things in response to death – anger, sadness and worry. But that worry does not predict reality.

Just because we worry about something, or we do not want something to happen, does not mean we think it into being. Thoughts and fears around death are normal, however they are rarely grounded in reality – they are more likely grounded in a fear of the unknown or the unpredictable.

Sit with your child, remind them that talking can help, that you also are struggling with some of these feelings and that fearing the unknown is something all people feel, even big people. The unknown removes all control from us and that can be a frightening abyss to stare into, but it really is just that – unknown – so that by probability it's just as likely to hold something wonderful as it is to hold something to fear.

DIFFERENT TYPES OF LOSS AND HOW TO HELP CHILDREN TO GRIEVE

Parental / sibling loss

There will likely be no loss bigger to a child than that of a parent or a sibling. Do not say things like, 'They are in a better place now,' or, 'They wouldn't want you to be sad.' This is a monumental loss, and it should be treated with reverence and respect. This loss will very likely be a significant life marker for a child and they will likely require professional support alongside good parenting to help them through the darkest parts. Charities such as Child Bereavement or Winston's Wish have amazing online resources to help you search for a professional in your area. This is not a loss that should be dealt with by the parents / remaining parent alone, due to the complexity of the grief and the potential impact on child mental health. However, don't feel the need to jump to calling in a professional too early on; many children want to speak in the first few days, weeks or months to a trusted adult. The key for successful therapy is willingness to engage and this often requires time.

Some things you can do:

- Explain the idea that grief is not a linear process – it will not feel the same every day and it will not look the same. Some days it will be all they can think and other days it will seem a small pinprick in their consciousness. That is OK! That does not mean the love felt was any less or that the person has been forgotten; that is the process of grief.
- All emotions are welcome, children do not have to feel sad every day to demonstrate their love or loss – they are allowed to feel happy, excited about things unrelated to the loss, and they are allowed to feel angry with the situation or the deceased. All of these things are welcome – and these emotions will likely need to be worked through with a professional.
- Allow them to help choose someone to talk to, explain the idea to them of counselling or grief support and let them have some say in the circumstances of how the person is engaged.
- If the child wants to return to school or after-school activities, let them. Do not project your own ideas around what the right time is for children to take off to grieve. Let them guide the process, but remind them that they can take a break any time they need. Remember grief is not linear.
- If you suspect that the child is showing PTSD-type reactions as a result of a death, EMDR therapy, Trauma

Focused CBT or Narrative Exposure Therapy are all evidence-based treatments that may help. Please see the resources section (page 223) for further details around different types of evidence based therapies for trauma.

- Emotional outbursts or behaviour changes are normal following this type of loss – the key here is to maintain boundaries and discipline with compassion. Yes, you can be compassionate to their loss, but you must remember that your role as parent is to keep them safe, and that means that while they may feel chaotic or in turmoil inside, this cannot extend to putting themselves or others in danger.

Miscarriage / pregnancy loss

Children under 12 will be unlikely to grasp what a miscarriage means or why sadly some pregnancies do not go to term. In this example, it can be helpful to simply say 'the baby has died'. You can also say, 'We have some very sad news, the doctors have examined the baby and they found the baby wasn't very strong and he has stopped breathing.'

In the case of premature birth or stillbirth, you can explain to younger children that the baby was 'born too early and he / she couldn't survive'. In the case of older children it is important to reassure them that 'Mummy is going to be OK and it doesn't mean anything is wrong with me, it's simply that the baby didn't develop in the womb properly.'

Children might want to remember the baby by having a special box that they can place memories in for them, or they might want to draw a picture or write a letter to the baby. If it feels important, or the loss was very traumatic, you can choose to mark what would have been the birthday every year, or whatever feels relevant to your family. There is no right or wrong way for a family to recover from pregnancy loss.

I have worked with families who wanted to name their baby or to create a special anniversary to mark their baby's presence in their lives. Other women have wanted to keep some of their maternity wear or baby clothes as a memento of their pregnancy, others have wanted to remind themselves of their child through a special piece of jewellery or stone. It's important to remember that marking your experience does not mean you are holding on to the past in an unhealthy way; you are acknowledging your emotions and experience in a compassionate act. You do not have to forget to heal.

Death / expected death as a result of illness

Sometimes due to the nature of the illness, such as cancer, we are informed of the likelihood of death prior to it. Families often ask, is this the time to tell children? My answer would always be yes, do not assume children will not pick up on signals of terminal illness becoming more degenerative, such as increased hospital appointments or visible signs of sickness. Offering them the space to process the idea that X will die is an important part of their grieving process.

As with other explanations we have gone through about death, stick to the facts: 'X's cancer has spread and the doctors have said they can't do anything else to treat it. They really wanted to and they really have tried everything they can. There is nothing you could have done about this.' They may have a lot of questions about what the doctors have done and why they can't do more: answer as much as you can but don't be afraid to say 'I don't know'.

Children don't have the same understanding as adults of illness and disease, and younger children in particular might need reassurance around 'catching' or 'getting' cancer. Fear is a natural response to the unknown and children often feel overwhelmed by these big topics and the concept that 'no one can cure this'. Both young children and teens may find some small comfort in caretaking as best they can for the dying person, even if this means writing a card or bringing in their favourite snacks; it can be relieving, if only for a short while, to 'do' something for the person. Let your child or teen help in whatever they want to; offer them space alone with their dying relative if they want it, but do not force this as some children find being in the presence of severe illness very frightening.

Death of a pet

This type of loss is often children's first experience of death and it can be devastating. A pet is for many a beloved family member and as animal lifespans are significantly shorter than that of humans it is not uncommon for children to have multiple experiences of pet loss. Explain the death in the same way you would a human: 'X has died.' Animals rarely have the same drawn-out deaths that humans do when they get sick, so the death may be very sudden. It is also likely to occur at home and the child may be there to witness it.

- Allow the child to grieve for the pet in the same way they would a human family member; allow them to help with any funeral arrangements and create any kind of memento that helps them to mark the pet's significance in their life.

- Share with your child that 'while X didn't speak our language, he knew how much you loved him'.
- Remind them that 'X had a wonderful life, he was surrounded by his favourite treats, walks and people who loved him'.
- Do not be offended or shocked if your child expresses anger or a sudden wish to get a new pet – this is a common child response to avoid feeling sadness, and it can be helpful to discuss this with them.

GRIEF-PROCESSING ACTIVITIES FOR CHILDREN

The memory box

Take a wooden box or shoebox with a lid and ask your child to decorate it. You can join in with them or give them the space to do this alone if they want. Invite them to place inside the memory box any tokens or reminders that feel special to them when they think about this person or this animal. It can also be a good time to invite children to put anything into the box they wish the person would know or could have.

As your child places something in the box, ask them why they have chosen it and what it means to them. Use this as a way to help them to express their feelings of loss.

One-more-minute star

This activity involves drawing or cutting out a star from paper or cardboard.

Upon this star, you can ask your child or teen to write down or represent in a drawing on the five points of the star:

1. Something you would like to say to the person if they had one more minute.
2. Something they would like to do with them if they had one more minute.
3. Something they would like to tell, that they didn't know, if they had one more minute.
4. Something good that has happened since they have gone.
5. A memory that reminds them of that person.

Write the person's name on the back and ask your child where they would like to keep the star.

The inside-out person

This activity is really helpful for when you think children or teens are holding a large amount of emotion inside and you think it might be helpful for them to talk about this with you or someone else. First draw a body. On the outside of the body, get the child to write down or help them to write down all the words that other people would say about them, in other words 'how others see me'. On the inside of the body, ask them to write down all the words people can't see about them: how they feel inside. Lastly, get your child to draw or use a coloured pen to

213

represent the emotions they have inside and mark on the body 'where they live'.

All the people in my world

Ask your child to draw themselves in the centre of the page. Invite them to draw all the people in their world who care for them. Instruct the child to draw them as close to the drawing of themselves as they feel so you can say, 'Put the people that love you the most closest to you (pointing at their drawing of them).' The purpose of this exercise is to help the child see that they have lots of people in their world who love and care for them. If your child is struggling to think of people beyond their immediate family, you can offer suggestions such as names of friends or extended family members or teachers.

HOW TO TALK TO NEURODIVERSE CHILDREN ABOUT DEATH

- ADHD children are often in possession of wonderful creative and imaginative skills. They may then find a lot of comfort in using these skills to help them understand or articulate their feelings about death or loss.
- ADHD children may be avoidant of certain emotions such as fear or sadness and for this reason, in response to bad news they may engage in behaviours that appear inappropriate or incongruent with a situation. Encourage them to not mask these emotions and to be open to the idea of expressing them in a way they feel comfortable – creative metaphor can feel a wonderful

way for ADHD children to express themselves without feeling overwhelmed by attempting to articulate their inner state.

- ASC children will likely have a number of questions about death and why it occurs; ASC children find safety in the known and danger in the unknown, so giving answers that are philosophical or vague can be irritating to them. Offer clear, concrete explanations such as 'his heart stopped', and allow room for questions.
- Don't assume a child with ASC will process information or distressing emotions as fast as a neurotypical person can – they may need a lot more time than you think to absorb this information in its entirety.
- Offer lots of space and comfort, remembering that ASC people find huge fear in the unknown and may need more comfort in this area, and less comfort in the area of processing negative emotion such as sadness.
- Don't be offended if your ASC child processes death in a way that appears cold or distant – their brains work at a logical level and abstract concepts such as grief can be confusing to them.

CONCLUSION

So, as we come to the ending, I reflect on something that has become my mantra throughout my therapy work: 'A good ending is therapy well done.' Early on in my career, my mentor told me that 'the ending of therapy is where the real work happens'. I have thought about this so much over the years and have come to realise that if I do nothing else as a therapist, I can aim to offer a good 'ending' to someone. Because life has a way of creating some terrible endings. Bereavements, sudden illness, friendship breakups, divorce, terminations of jobs: life often chooses an 'ending' for you, and in these abrupt and unchosen endings many of our most traumatic memories are stored. So, where possible in my work, I try to create meaningful endings, endings whereby people can reflect upon and appreciate the experience they have had. To end something well helps someone to integrate the experience and also to move beyond the experience. I like to remind my patients and my children to give themselves permission to experience a long ending. Don't be so keen to push it to one side and think on to the next – spend time reflecting on what this has meant, mark it in some way, don't run away from the emotion the ending is bringing up; let that breathe. An ending well spent is a memory well stored.

Life – with its way of creating difficult endings – also has a way of creating the bumps and bruises that we have in this book called small t traumas. No one comes through life without the captain turning on the seatbelt sign to signify turbulence at least once. We would all love to prevent our children from ever feeling hurt or fear or shame, but we can't. We can, however, seek to help them integrate these experiences into their memory in a way that serves them. We can give space to emotions that come up during traumatic moments, we can sit with – rather than run away from – these unsettled feelings of turbulence, we can offer space for endings.

I hope you will begin to integrate the idea of extract–express–reflect into your journey as a parent and even as a friend or partner. Allowing someone the space to process the facts (extract), voice the emotion (express) and consolidate the experience in a meaningful way (reflect) helps them to move beyond what has happened, and to grow with it. This three-step process doesn't need you to be a therapist, a neuroscientist or a trauma expert, it just needs you to be able to ask, listen and reflect. I hope that you will find ways to incorporate this technique into your lives to help your loved ones integrate their experiences into their lives.

To be a therapist has been one of the greatest blessings of my life. To have been gifted the experience to bear witness to so many stories and to have been entrusted to hear both the best of humanity and the worst of it, has been an honour for which I will be forever thankful. I have had the privilege of working with hundreds of people, children and adults, and I feel a deep love for all of them. I think something that might surprise you about therapists is the amount our patients mean to us. I can say without exaggeration that I have loved every soul I have worked with. I find myself mentally willing them on from the side lines as I think about their stories, and I feel more joy for their wins and pain for their losses than they probably realise. But that is what happens when you truly empathise with another's story and say, 'I hear you, I see you, you matter.'

My patients come to me to share the sad, difficult, shameful and unloved parts of themselves and ask me to help them 'fix' it – and in my early career I so desperately wanted to do this. I never wanted to admit that sometimes I didn't know how. I felt as lost in the confusion and the hopelessness as they did. What I have come to realise is that the biggest gift you can bestow on another is to say, 'I see all of the chaos and the destruction, I will meet you there.' All of us in life want someone to stand next to us. We don't always need a fixer, someone to make it right, someone to tell us what to do – we need someone to say, 'In a place where you don't have the answers, wait for me, I am coming.' In so many ways, the things I have learnt that make me a better therapist – the benefit of listening rather than jumping in, the gift of 'presence' rather than panicked action, and the act of truly empathising – have made me a better parent.

Becoming a mother has been such an overwhelming, magical, frustrating, heart-breaking and joyous experience that I wouldn't have the words to describe it all. If you asked me what were the top five moments of my life, all of them would be within the years I have become a parent, but that doesn't take away from the fact that being a parent has been incredibly hard. Parenting is humbling, it is enraging, it is eternally challenging. You are passed the biggest responsibility of your life, with no training, no guidebook and what feels like – in the darkest moments – no help. Parenting has ripped me apart and built me back up more times than I care to remember. Recently my youngest child said to me, 'You don't love me,' and I felt completely deflated. 'I love you so much it hurts,' I thought ragefully. 'I love you so much I feel like I might burst inside with the weight of it.' Of course, my daughter was using a five-year-old's tactic of saying something spiteful in response to her own rage about being told she couldn't have the snack she asked for, but my internal response was such a storm of emotions I felt like I was drowning. However, using all my skills as a therapist I quelled the storm and told her, 'I will love you forever, but that's not what we were talking about, we were talking about snacks.'

As parents we are faced every day with this emotional tsunami: the feeling of loving our child alongside the parental responsibility of 'raising' our child. Parenting can indeed show us the parts of ourselves that we don't love, and maybe that have never felt loved, and that we might have spent a long time hiding from the world. But parenting also likely shows you the resilient parts, the brave parts and the compassionate parts that you have maybe also hidden from the world. There is a theory in psychoanalytic psychology called a 'golden shadow'. It is the gold we have within ourselves that we 'see' in others; it is the bravery, the kindness, the strength that for whatever reason we don't like to own. I imagine if you look through your own parenting journey you will find these examples in your story. Just as we do in the extract–express–reflect technique, if you take a moment to sit back and think about your parenting journey, where are the parts that YOU can be proud of?

Ask yourself what this journey has taught you. When doing this, be brave enough to avoid the voices in your head that say you 'should have done / could have done more or less of . . .' and listen to the real lessons parenting has given you. Just as if we were doing extract–express–reflect, look for the facts, remembering that your thoughts are not facts; facts are demonstrable evidence. Ask yourself, is my child safe? Is my child loved? If your gut is telling you to answer no to either of these questions, look for the facts that support this or those that say otherwise. Parenting often throws us into turmoil where we feel we have to *do more* and *do better,* when in reality our child is doing just fine. We are constantly barraged by messages about how to raise children, but my advice is this: if your child is safe and loved, your role as a parent has been fulfilled to the highest purpose.

Now let's reflect: what do you feel about being a parent? This question often makes us rush to an answer of, 'Oh it's the best thing in my life.' But that's the voices in your head again trying to take over. Really sit with the question and think: what do you FEEL? A feeling is not a fact, it is an experience. If the answer is inadequate / lost / exhausted – that's OK. If the answer is a mixture of inadequate / lost / exhausted *and* elated / blessed / delighted, then – wonderful. When we can own our feelings without judgement, we help our child do the same. We don't have to feel joy and gratitude for every minute of our parenting journey, and your child doesn't have to feel joy and gratitude for every moment of their childhood. What we can aim for is creating a feeling of safety and love. They can be in complete turmoil and so can you, but love endures. When love endures, safety follows.

All of this is not easy; parents are preconditioned to feel uncomfortable in celebrating themselves as parents. We often say things like, 'I could do more, I wish I had done . . .' We feel ashamed of saying, 'I am proud of this.' If parents take anything from this book, I hope they take this: if you choose to parent with the intention to keep your child safe and to love them, you have done a wonderful job; if your child can come to you when they feel sad, lost, ashamed or chaotic, then you, my friend, have done a wonderful job.

Children don't need you to be perfect, they don't need you to know every answer, they don't need you to be infallible. They need a space they can hold in their heart as safe: that space is you. They need somewhere they can come back to when they are done exploring, when they have fallen down, and when they are hurt or embarrassed. They need somewhere a hug is waiting with no questions asked; they need a place where all of them is welcome. A place where, when they don't have the answers, compassion will be waiting.

You don't have to be a perfect parent, you just have to be there when their travels get too much, when their flights of independence feel too far, saying: 'In all of the chaos of life, wait for me, I am coming.'

RESOURCES

RECOMMENDED READING

Walker, Pete, *Complex PTSD: From Surviving to Thriving: A Guide and Map for Recovering from Childhood Trauma* (CreateSpace Independent Publishing Platform: 2013)

Brain development

Mate, Gabor, *Scattered Minds: The Origins and Healing of Attention Deficit Disorder* (Vintage Canada: 2000)
Siegel, Daniel J. and Payne Bryson, Tina, *The Whole-Brain Child* (Robinson: 2012)

Trauma

Levine, Peter A., *Waking the Tiger: Healing Trauma: The Innate Capacity to Transform Overwhelming Experiences* (North Atlantic Books: 1997)
Rothschild, Babette, *The Body Remembers: The Psychophysiology*

of Trauma and Trauma Treatment (W. W. Norton & Company: 2000)

Van Der Kolk, Bessel, *The Body Keeps the Score* (Penguin: 2015)

Survivors of abuse

Sanderson, Christine, *The Warrior Within a One in Four Handbook to Aid Recovery from Childhood Sexual Abuse and Violence* (One in Four: 2013)

Winfrey, Oprah, and Perry, Bruce, *What Happened to You? Conversations on Trauma, Resilience, and Healing* (Bluebird: 2021)

USEFUL WEBSITES

www.emdr.com
www.thebowencenter.org
www.ptsduk.org
www.talkgrief.org
www.nspcc.org.uk
www.nctsn.org
www.youngminds.org.uk

Psychology tools including find a therapist

www.bacp.co.uk
www.hcpc-uk.org
www.psychotherapy.org.uk
www.apa.org
www.psychology.org.au

ACKNOWLEDGEMENTS

Thank you first and foremost to my editor Jess and my agent Lauren. Thank you for believing in me and the vision I had for this book; none of these words would be on a page without your unwavering support. I am deeply grateful for the passion you showed in bringing this book to life and for taking a chance on the psychologist who didn't know how to use TikTok.

Thank you also to the wonderful team at Orion for being so dedicated and engaged in this project, and for generously sharing your advice and thoughts.

Thank you to my mentor Pete Holloway, whose wisdom I have shared many times within these pages and whose words have carried me through many of my own toughest moments. I am so honoured to be able to share your words with others.

To Eleanor Zeal, my love always.

To Ed Shen, who I know doesn't read anything but Freud . . . hopefully you will see this, thank you.

To Clare James for being a fellow witch, wise woman and a wonderful therapist.

Thank you to my personal cheerleading team: Ashley, Jaime

and Joanna, who all individually reminded me why I should write this book and never tired of boosting my confidence to put myself out there. All of you personify the beauty of female friendship and the true meaning of a girl squad.

To my dear friend and colleague Arthur Fang, who has always been there to offer a wise ear and a proofreading eye!

Thank you to my parents Ian and Lynne, my family Laura, Raff, Maxi and Bastien.

To M, to girl A, and to my garden of yellow flowers, for always keeping me safe and reminding me to be a safe space to others. My heart loves you.

No acknowledgments section would be space enough to give thanks to the greatest person I know, my beloved husband, David, without whom I wouldn't be a therapist, a mother and definitely not a published writer. To quote Rumi, with you I intend to 'laugh as much as I breathe and love as long as I live'.

Of course, finally, my beautiful girls, Tabitha and Isobel. Thank you for making me a mother, teaching me what it is to be a mother, and blessing me every day just by being you. My love always and forever.

INDEX

Page numbers in *italic* refer to figures.